AT THE COALFACE

To my esteemed colleagues, past and present, in the Archdiocese of Dublin

J. Anthony Gaughan

At The Coalface

RECOLLECTIONS OF
A CITY AND COUNTRY PRIEST
1950-2000

the columba press

First published in 2000 by
the columba press
55A Spruce Avenue, Stillorgan Industrial Park,
Blackrock, Co Dublin

Cover by Bill Bolger
Origination by The Columba Press
Printed in Ireland by Colour Books Ltd, Dublin

ISBN 1 85607 315 7

Acknowledgements

Michael O'Carroll, CSSp, published *A priest in changing times* in 1998. Kevin H. Donlon, CSsR, saw his *And ink be on their hands* come out a year later. I derived considerable encouragement and pleasure from the recollections of these two very talented priest-friends. It occurred to me that my reflections from a different perspective might also be interesting and useful: hence this book.

In connection with its preparation I wish to thank all who jogged my memory, not least the colleagues with whom I had and have the honour of serving in various parishes.

I am indebted to Fr Noel Barber, SJ, Tadhg O'Carroll, Peter O'Keeffe, Pat O'Kelly, David Sheehy and especially Maurice O'Connell for much helpful criticism.

I am grateful to Mrs Eileen Francis for preparing the manuscript for publication.

I feel very honoured in having the Foreword provided by Cardinal Cahal B. Daly.

Finally, I am delighted to have the book published by The Columba Press.

J. Anthony Gaughan
1 July 2000

Contents

Foreword

Cardinal Cahal B. Daly

It is a pleasure to contribute a foreword to this book by a priest who has succeeded in combining a busy and fruitful parish ministry with an impressive literary output. Many of Father Gaughan's publications have required a great deal of research, of a scale which would normally be associated with a fulltime academic posting; but his writings have been researched and seen through the press with no derogation whatever from full pastoral duties, and without benefit of sabbaticals. This is a rare achievement.

All this speaks eloquently of the author's dedication to all aspects of his priestly calling to the ministry of Word and Sacrament. Father Gaughan would not permit of any incompatibility between his literary work and his pastoral work. Both are at the service of truth; both are part of the dialogue between faith and reason for which Pope John Paul has pleaded in his 1998 encyclical, *Fides et Ratio;* both spring from the same love of the church.

It is refreshing to read the present well-written and enthusiastic account of one priest's experience 'at the coal face' of parish pastoral life in a wide variety of parishes and social situations in city and country, throughout a half-century of profound change in the church and in society. It is interesting and at the same time amusing to read his sometimes wry but never malicious comments on confrères and superiors, his honest but never unkind observations on social snobbery in some parishes, pomposity in some persons, but sheer goodness and true holiness in unexpected places and people.

This book gives us a glimpse of the variety of gifts and qualities required of Irish diocesan priests, and of their dedication to their priestly tasks and their readiness for new challenges. This book points also to the fraternity and camaraderie which bind diocesan priests together as a diocesan team, and which help to counter-act any inclinations to give in to loneliness and self-pity. The book gives us a picture of a body of priests who, whatever their failings and foibles and their all too human faults, do remain close to their people, while also seeking to remain close to God. They continue to give to their people a kind and a quality of un-selfish service which is rarely encountered in today's world, but which is rightly expected of priests whose paramount aim in life is the service of God's Kingdom. My feeling after reading Father Gaughan's text is that it is good to meet a priest who is happy and fulfilled in his priesthood, and who has found it, in his own words, 'very challenging but also rewarding beyond all expect-ations'. The message of this book is expressed in words which Father Gaughan appropriately quotes from Father Karl Rahner:

> If we are bound together, priest and people, then we already bear veiled in our midst, Jesus Christ, his grace and eternal life.

CHAPTER 1

Holy Cross College, Clonliffe
1950-1953

I was born in Listowel, County Kerry, on 19 August 1932. My father was Anthony Gaughan and my mother Kathleen (Dolly) Broderick, a native of the town. I attended the local national school and St Michael's College. The family was in business. We had a lounge bar, the 'Rendezvous', and a garage, 'Listowel Auto Services'. In addition we were agents for Powers of Waterford, the fish exporters. As I had neither brother nor sister, I had from my earliest years more than ample experience of these ventures.

From their school days with the Presentation Sisters my mother and aunt began each day by attending 8 o'clock Mass. Throughout their lives they had immense affection and even reverence for the Sisters. They also held in very high regard the local priests not so much for their undoubted commendable human qualities but for what they represented. Like many other people in the town I attended Mass during Lent and 'did the nine Fridays'. This was a devotion centred on the Sacred Heart of Jesus and involved going to Confession and Holy Communion on nine consecutive first Fridays.

On Sunday the family invariably attended first Mass which was at 8 o'clock. While the adults went by car I, as early as I can recall, always walked on my own to church, where I sat well away from the family. A spirit of independence on my part may have contributed to this practice but the main reason was peer pressure. Any young male seen at that time dutifully accompanying the grown-ups to Mass would be in disgrace!

Even from the pictures in the house we could be described as a stereo-type of the Irish Catholic family of that time. In the kitchen/dining-room, where we spent most of the day, there was a large picture of the Sacred Heart of Jesus with a bright red electric lamp in front of it and on the opposite wall was an equally large portrait of a handsome, youthful General Michael Collins

As my time at St Michael's was coming to an end there was an unspoken assumption that I would stay at home, help with the various businesses and eventually take them over. But I was determined to get away at least for a few years before doing so. To facilitate this, I had two professions in mind: primary-school teaching and the army. The first step into the teaching profession was a call to one of the Teacher Training Colleges. This required passing the 'Easter orals' which I managed, and after that entry was determined on the basis of performance in the Leaving Certificate.

As far as I was concerned, however, primary school-teaching was only a second option. My real ambition was to have a commission in the army. My father had been an officer in the Irish Free State army and my uncle-in-law, Captain Tom Shanahan, had spent most of his life in that service. Two of my friends at St Michael's, a distant cousin, Seán Kissane, later known as Jack Kissane when playing football for Galway, and Michael Mulcahy, had gone on to the cadet college in the Curragh. Michael Mulcahy, son of the local superintendent, next door neighbour and my closest friend, was just a year ahead of me at St Michael's and on the trips home during his first year in the cadet college was loud in his praise of it.

Then out of the blue my grandmother, Mrs Elizabeth Broderick, who resided with us, asked me what I intended to do after the Leaving Certificate marks had arrived. I told her. She then enquired had I considered studying for the priesthood. Probably because I had not been an altar boy, nobody had ever put that question to me. Perhaps I had been waiting for the question. 1950 had been designated a Holy Year and the Listowel Boy Scouts, of which I was a member, went on a pilgrimage to Rome. At a general audience with Pope Pius XII our scoutmaster, Michael Kennelly, handed a gift on our behalf to the pope for the peoples of war-torn Europe. The audience was memorable as were other aspects of the pilgrimage.

In any case, as a result of the challenging question, I went up to Canon David O'Connor, president of St Michael's, and told him I had decided at least 'to have a shot at studying for the priesthood'. He was obviously not impressed by this show of bravado. Irascible and with an appallingly-choleric temperament to cope with, David was not a popular person. Stemming from him, a very harsh discipline prevailed throughout St Michael's. Notwithstanding this, he was respected in the community at large. He had genuine sympathy for the poor and the under-privileged and he ensured that any boy in the town or its vicinity who could profit from second-level education was given the opportunity to have it. His sincerity and total commitment to his responsibilities at St Michael's, as well as his irrational determination that, as he was wont to say, 'my boys' would gain extraordinary marks in the public examinations were also widely acknowledged and appreciated.

The president asked me if there was any diocese or religious order in which I wished to serve as a priest. I replied that I had none in mind. He then told me that his friend, Fr Bob Walsh, was in Dublin diocese and always spoke highly of it. So he had me sit down and draft a request for admission to Holy Cross College, Clonliffe. 'The priest', as we referred to him, crossly pointed out a misspelling. He then drafted the application, had me copy it and I sent it off.

In due course I received an invitation to an interview in Clonliffe College and was requested to bring my marks in the Leaving Certificate. I had never seen a major or indeed any kind of seminary before and I was amazed at how beautiful and imposing the college and the grounds were. The college had been founded in 'Clonliffe House' by Archbishop (later Cardinal) Paul Cullen in 1859, and transferred into the seminary which was completed in 1863. The college church of the Holy Cross was added in 1876. In 1951 a new wing was built and there were further extensions in 1958 and 1960.

The interview was my first meeting with Canon John Kelly,

president of the college. Although he had been born and raised in Liverpool, his accent was only slightly anglicised. His manner was gruff and peremptory, which was his way of covering up an almost pathological shyness. He exuded manliness and, as I later learned, he was an excellent scholar and lecturer in theology. At the interview all he seemed interested in were my marks in the Leaving Certificate.

In less than a week I had a letter to report to Holy Cross College, Clonliffe. It included a list of the requirements I was to bring with me. These included: (1) a black suit, white shirt, black tie, black shoes and socks and a black coat and hat; (2) a soutanne, Roman collar and biretta; and (3) a soprano and Roman hat. The first items were for outdoor wear and the second were worn in the college. The third items were eye-catching. The suprano was an ornate soutanne with long crimson stripes. The Roman hat can still be seen worn by clerics in Rome. This was a step down from the *haut couture* of a few years earlier when the required head-gear was a top hat! These third items were worn by Clonliffe students as we walked in procession, two by two, to and from the Pro-Cathedral on Sundays and in Holy Week and Easter week to take part in ceremonies.

The list also included a Bible, St Francis de Sales' *Introduction to the devout life* and Thomas a Kempis' *The imitation of Christ*. During my first year in Clonliffe I set out to read the Bible from beginning to end. Somewhere in the middle of the Old Testament I gave up and I never afterwards succeeded in doing so. *Introduction to the devout life* was a quaint book with many archaic words and replete with imagery and examples from the world of nature. I found neither the Old Testament nor St Francis de Sales' alleged classic on spirituality attractive. However, I enjoyed Thomas a Kempis. His was a book full of enlightened common sense and enduring aphorisms. One I liked to quote was: 'Many a merry evening maketh a sad morning'.

Just two days after the 30 or so of us arrived to begin study for the priesthood we were launched into the 'Thirty Days' retreat which was based on the spiritual exercises of St Ignatius

Loyola, founder of the Jesuits. Fr Bobby Nash, SJ, directed it. At the time he was a well-known retreat-giver and had begun his long career of writing books on prayer and spirituality. Already, he had written a few books of meditations for priests and religious. One of them *The priest at his priedieu* most of us equipped ourselves with at the end of the retreat.

Bobby Nash took the retreat very seriously, as he did himself. We had four lectures each day, based on incidents in the life of Christ, much reflection and meditation, a great deal of spiritual reading – the lives of the saints, etc. – as well as the normal spiritual exercises in the college: Mass, visit to the Blessed Sacrament, Rosary and morning and evening prayers. Except for three days, a strict silence was observed throughout the retreat, even at meal times. Bobby Nash did not hesitate to challenge our youthful enthusiasm and idealism. One of the key meditations was entitled 'The two standards' and he left us in no doubt as to what standard we were to follow. He had a profound influence on all of us. Thus he told us that smoking and alcohol were luxuries and so should have no place in the life of a priest. For decades afterwards most of us never smoked or drank alcohol. I vividly remember some of his repetitive phrases: 'a holy priest makes a holy people, a priest who is not holy is not only useless but harmful'; and 'Thou art a priest forever, according to the order of Melchisadech'. Nash's lectures were never boring and he was at his most interesting when weaving into them stories about the heroism of fellow-Jesuit, Fr Willie Doyle, a famous army chaplain in World War I.

Unlike my companions from the country who had been boarders in diocesan colleges, I had never lived away from home. Yet I was surprised at how home-sick I was on a few occasions, although one of them was intelligible enough. During the summer I had been a member of the Kerry minor football squad. They eventually met and defeated a Wexford team in the final in Croke Park on the third Sunday of September. On that Sunday afternoon after one of the lectures I went out strolling in the grounds. The senior game between Mayo and Louth was in

progress. Not only could the loud cheering be heard but when
the football was kicked high in the air I could see it from the college grounds, as the first Hogan stand was quite a low structure.
I felt very sorry for myself. (Four years later in similar circumstances I was fortunate to be a Maynooth rather than a Clonliffe
student, see Appendix 1.)

At that time students for the priesthood in Dublin were
required to have graduated with a primary degree before pro-
gressing to theology. From mid-October onwards we cycled in
pairs across the city to lectures in UCD, then at Earlsfort Terrace.
First Arts was much like the Leaving Certificate, except for one
subject, Logic and introduction to philosophy. Quite a few of the
professors and lecturers were coming to the end of their
academic careers and it showed. At his lectures An tOllamh
Cormac Ó Cadhlaigh with scarcely a glance at the attendance
read a few chapters of his study of Irish grammar *Gnás na
Gaeilge*. With hardly a comment Dr Roger McHugh in his lectures
on one of Shakespeare's plays had students read the dialogue of
the various characters. Mícheál Ó hAodha was leader of the Fine
Gael group in Seanad Éireann, a key figure in the Fine Gael
political organisation and his first subject was French language
and literature: factors which no doubt explained his disappointing
performance as a lecturer on Irish. Máire Mac an tSaoi, and Dr
Lorna Reynolds were equally unimpressive in their respective
Irish and English seminars.

Professor Dudley Edwards of the history department was a
'character' and he knew it. There were stories about his clown-
ing around college. Over six feet and built in proportion he had
a magnificent head with a hair style like Einstein. His facial
expression was that of a person who had just been startled and
his voice was squeaky and high-pitched. His approach to his
lectures was idiosyncratic. He did not lecture in the accepted
academic sense but merely posed numerous unconnected questions which prompted us to think. In the second term he had
Miriam McDonnell, who was studying for her MA, deliver his
lectures while he presided. My chief recollection of the third

term was that on a number of warm, sunny days he told us to take up our chairs and follow him out into Iveagh Gardens. There as we sat around him Dudley would read the daily newspaper and urge us to be critical of its contents! It may be that Dudley's antics were what we needed at that time. In any event they did not seem to have a negative effect on at least three of my fellow-students in First Arts history: Brian Farrell, Louis MacRedmond and Ronan Keane who subsequently had remarkably successful careers.

In 1980, I had reason to respect Dudley's utter disregard for public opinion. Miriam McDonnell had become Mrs James Daly and both she and her husband had appointments in Queen's University, Belfast. Miriam, who was a prominent member of the Irish Republican Socialist Party, was assassinated by loyalists in her home. James and their two children came to see me and asked me to celebrate a memorial Mass for Miriam in Mount Merrion, her home parish, for relatives and friends. I was glad to oblige James with whom I had been acquainted when he had been a student at Maynooth for the archdiocese of Armagh. The congregation was very different from the usual one I faced at Mount Merrion. In addition there was a liberal sprinkling of members of the Special Branch and of journalists. Just as I was about to begin Dudley walked briskly up to the front seat and knelt beside James and the two children.

Fr Tom Dunning, CM, and Rev Professor E. F. O'Doherty were the two outstanding lecturers in First Arts. In the course on English Dunning gave a splendid series of lectures on the philippics of Edmund Burke. Nearly all the students, lay as well as clerical, took O'Doherty's lectures on logic and introduction to philosophy and, as a result, he had to hold these in an overcrowded Physics theatre, the largest lecture theatre available.

After First Arts, Clonliffe students preparing for the Pass BA took philosophy and another subject, while honours students read philosophy. The philosophy course included metaphysics (epistemology, natural theology and ontology); logic and psychology: ethics and politics; and history of philosophy. The faculty members: Rev Professor John Horgan (metaphysics), Rev Professor E. F. O'Doherty (logic and psychology), Rev Professor Conor Martin (ethics), Canon Denis O'Keeffe (politics) and Fr Bertie Crowe (history of philosophy): came to their lectures punctually, prepared and with enthusiasm. The lectures of O'Doherty and Martin were always very good and frequently inspiring. Although the course was centred on Thomism, it was comprehensive, including a treatment in one or other of the various disciplines of all the great philosophers and thinkers from Plato and Aristotle to A. J. Ayer, Sigmund Freud, Carl Gustav Jung, Bertrand Russell, Ludwig Wittgenstein and the Existentialists.

I was fascinated by philosophy, enjoyed the lectures, availed of every opportunity to read widely on the subject and reflected a great deal on what I read. All the hard work I put into my stud-ies paid off. In Second Arts I managed 1st class honours in all subjects and a university scholarship and in the BA examination a double first and a post-graduate scholarship.

We were directed when attending UCD not to become involved in student activities nor even to mingle with the lay students. This last we regarded as merely an indication not to loiter in the corri-dors between lectures. Thus we spent time at Earlsfort Terrace either at lectures or studying in the library. The various societies and sports facilities in the university were replicated, albeit feebly, in Clonliffe. We had a debating society. A play was pres-ented annually. There were a number of societies promoting various hobbies. In the first term a soccer league and in the second a Gaelic football league were organised. The Gaelic football league was initiated in 1944 after the secretary of the GAA, Paddy O'Keeffe, who resided on Clonliffe Road, persuaded the authorities to allow Gaelic football in the college. A few times a year a very competitive soccer match between senior house, the theologians, and junior house, the philosophers – those attend-ing UCD – was played. There were also facilities for playing croquet and tennis in the summer.

The routine in Clonliffe for the 65 or so philosophers and the

50 theologians was demanding. The daily *horarium* or timetable except for Saturday and Sunday was:

6.00 Rise
6.20 Morning Prayer
6.30 Meditation (in oratory or room)
7.00 Mass
7.45 Breakfast and Recreation
9.00 Study
9.30 to 2.45, except for a tea-break, class and study periods
2.45 Visit to Blessed Sacrament
3.00 Dinner and Recreation
5.00 Study
7.00 Spiritual Reading
7.30 Tea and Recreation
8.30 Study
9.30 Night Prayer
10.00 Lights out

The theological training in the college was conducted by Canon John Kelly (president/professor of dogmatic theology), Rev Dr Edward Gallen (vice-president and professor of canon law), Fr Michael Clarke (professor of moral theology), Fr Joseph Carroll (professor of sacred scripture) and Fr Cathal McCarthy (dean and professor of liturgy).

In Clonliffe the only priest the philosophers had much dealings with was Fr Cathal McCarthy. By definition the dean of a college is not popular. Nor did Cathal do much to enhance himself to us either. He was pompous, his facial expression was usually one of disdain and he had more than an ordinary capacity for sarcasm. In fairness though, it must be stated that he was also a man of remarkable courage and determination; returning to his post after suffering horrific injuries when knocked down by a car on the main road near the college.

In our first year we had a very useful weekly class on liturgy from Cathal, who had few equals in his subject. He also had us buy a copy of *Courtesy for clerics*. This was a compendium of every conceivable convention with regard to courtesy, etiquette and politeness. It was by an anonymous author. Although it was stated that Cathal was the real author, this was never confirmed. Cathal also gave us a number of lectures in courtesy! His aim was to produce 'Christian gentlemen' but I am afraid that after three years, probably because of the poor material he had to work on, all he had was a bunch of young men with just the slightest veneer of sophistication.

In our third year we had a weekly lecture on the Old Testament from Joe Carroll which was quite interesting.

There was a set procedure at that time for allocating students to different institutions for theology after their BA year. More than half would remain in Clonliffe, from the remainder one, two or three would be sent to Rome, when places were available in the Irish College or that of Propaganda Fide, the rest would go to St Patrick's College, Maynooth. I enjoyed my time in Clonliffe – the study, football, camaraderie and through it all the routine of prayer. However, my personal order of preference for my location during the next four years was (1) either of the two colleges in Rome, (2) Maynooth and (3) remaining in Clonliffe. By that time I was finding life in Clonliffe rather restrictive. There was the seeming omnipresence of Cathal McCarthy. Symbolic of the undue attention to detail and trivia in the college was the fact that we had to wear the biretta during all our waking hours and not only that but to wear it properly! Once during recreation Cathal came up behind me and said: 'Mr Gaughan. You wear the biretta like a circus clown.'

In the event, Dick Lewis who had been our university prefect and was a very worthy person, was allocated the only vacancy in Rome that year. Unfortunately Dick had a breakdown in health and had to abandon his study for the priesthood after just two years in Rome. With five others I was sent to Maynooth. I was very pleased with the posting.

CHAPTER 2

St Patrick's College, Maynooth
1953-1957

Of the six Clonliffe students allocated to Maynooth three of us sat for the honours BA examination in the autumn. Consequently we were granted a concession of not reporting to the college until the second week in October.

I had much to learn about this famous institution of which Mgr Patrick J. Corish gave the following overview in his *Maynooth College: 1795-1995* (Dublin 1995):

> Maynooth College was founded in 1795 when revolutionary developments in Europe had closed the continental seminaries. During the seventeenth and eighteenth centuries, the Catholic Church in Ireland had developed a network of these seminaries. With their closure a very large replacement programme in Ireland was needed. It suited the government to help and the foundation of Maynooth College was made possible by Act of Parliament in 1795.
>
> Maynooth rapidly developed into a seminary larger than any that had existed before. By 1853, it was claimed that more than half the priests of Ireland had been educated at Maynooth. The continuing growth of the student body allowed it to develop university status – two universities, in fact, one with a pontifical charter in 1896 and the second as a 'recognised college' of the National University of Ireland in 1910.
>
> For two hundred years, therefore, Maynooth has played a pivotal role within the Catholic Church in Ireland. Reflecting the political and social evolution of Ireland itself, and mirroring separate theological developments within the church, the

history of Maynooth has rarely been tranquil, occasionally fractious but always influential.

Today Maynooth has developed from its modest beginning as a seminary for a handful of priests into a major university with 4,000 students, the majority of them lay men and women.

In 1954-5 the college had 555 students. The student body was made up as follows: Dunboyne post-graduate students 21, theology students 271 and philosophy, arts and science students 263. By a remarkable coincidence the sum total of students in the following year was also 555. Nearly all of those had been the most promising pupils in the 23 minor seminaries throughout the country. The college staff could stand comparison with the staff of any third level institution of the same size anywhere in the world. The college buildings were equally impressive: Stoyte House and its extensions, the Gothic pile designed by Pugin and completed in 1850, the college chapel and tower and the early and later extensions.

Such was the spaciousness of the college grounds that one could frequently feel somewhat lost. There were the various squares and a large open area behind the college. Here there were over 20 football pitches, including the 'high field', where interclass Gaelic football and hurling matches were played. This area also had croquet and tennis courts for the various dioceses. Criss-crossing it were numerous walks, the main one 'Grafton', as wide as a public thoroughfare.

For the Dublin students, who had not been in a minor seminary, arrival in Maynooth was something of a culture shock. Suddenly we realised that there was more than one archdiocese and archbishop in the country. There were four archdioceses and twenty two dioceses besides! We became acutely aware that Maynooth was the very heart of the Irish Church, with nearly all the priests and most of the bishops of Ireland passing through its portals. A stroll through the cloister in senior house left me in no doubt in that regard. The walls featured large portraits of *alumni* who had been prelates in many of the archdioceses and dioceses of the country. Even more impressive were the class-pieces containing the photographs of the 70 or more priests ordained each year for service throughout Ireland.

Although the *horarium* or timetable in Maynooth did not differ significantly from that in Clonliffe there were subtle differences, especially in matters of discipline, dictated by the very large number of students. We adjusted to these very quickly and I have yet to meet a Dublin priest who has not expressed a preference for his years in Maynooth to those he spent in his original *alma mater*.

As a national institution Maynooth College had a colourful and varied history and each of the college buildings has many interesting historical associations. But the stories of the college's past which were most vividly remembered and passed on from one generation of students to another concerned Dunboyne House and the 'haunted room' in 'Rhetoric' in Junior House.

Dunboyne House had its origin in a bequest made in 1800 by John Butler, bishop of Cork, and twelfth Baron Dunboyne. Butler, the third son of the eighth Baron Dunboyne, was ordained a Catholic priest and later appointed bishop of Cork in 1763. On the death of his nephew in 1786 he succeeded to the Dunboyne title and the family estates. He resigned his see. Being the last surviving member of his family in the male line, he applied to the pope for permission to marry. This was refused and he conformed to the established Protestant religion and married a cousin, from which marriage there was no issue. Before his death in 1800 Dunboyne asked to be received back into the Catholic Church and in his last will bequeathed his property in County Meath to the trustees of Maynooth College. The validity of the will was contested and eventually the case was settled out of court with the trustees of the college accepting half the original annuity which was owing to them.

In his *Window on Maynooth* (Dublin 1949) Denis Meehan attempted to distinguish between fact and fiction in the college lore about the 'haunted room' as follows:

The two upper floors of Rhetoric House are altogether residential and the ghost-room is, or rather was, room no. 2 on the top corridor. It is now an oratory of St Joseph. Legend of course is rife concerning the history of this room; but unfortunately everything happened so long ago that one cannot now guarantee anything like accuracy. The incident, whatever it may have been, is at least dated to some extent by a trustees' resolution of October 23, 1860: 'That the president be authorised to convert room no. 2 on the top corridor of Rhetoric House into an oratory of St Joseph, and to fit up an oratory of St Aloysius in the prayer hall of the junior students.'

 The story, as it is commonly now retailed, for the edification of susceptible freshmen, begins with a suicide. The student resident in this room killed himself one night. According to some he used a razor; but tellers are not too careful about such details. The next inhabitant, it is alleged, felt irresistibly impelled to follow suit, and again, according to some, he did. A third, or it may have been the second, to avoid a similar impulse, and when actually about to use his razor, jumped through the window into Rhetoric yard. He broke some bones, but saved his life. Subsequently no student could be induced to use the room; but a priest volunteered to sleep or keep vigil there for one night. In the morning his hair was white, though no one dares to relate what his harrowing experiences can have been. Afterwards the front wall of the room was removed and a small altar of St Joseph was erected.

The basic details of the story have doubtless some found–ation in fact, and it is safe to assume that something very unpleasant did occur. The suicide (or suicides), in so far as one can deduce from the oral traditions that remain, seems to have taken place in the period 1842-48.

By the time my co-diocesan, Mick O'Donohue, and I arrived in the college, New House which was reserved for first year theologians was full. Consequently we were assigned a room in a small residential area on the ground floor of Long Corridor adjoining St Joseph's oratory. This section was rather appropriately known as 'Pigs'. The living conditions were Spartan even for those times. There was no water in the room and the only toilet to which we had access was an outdoor one which was generally in an appalling condition. To compound the situation the rest of Long Corridor was being demolished and the displaced rats were seeking refuge in our section of it.

Senior house which consisted of the BA year and the four theology years was divided into St Joseph's, with the BAs and first year theologians, and St Mary's, with the second, third and fourth year theologians. Fr James Cosgrove was the dean of St Joseph's. A native of County Cavan, of Kilmore diocese, he was ponderous in his walk and speech. One recognised immediately that he was a lover of the out-of-doors and that, if given a choice, would have opted for a curacy somewhere in County Cavan rather than being a dean in Maynooth. Subsequently he became college bursar and was successful and contented in that role.

'Cosie' or 'the sheriff' as we referred to him, checked that we were in St Joseph's oratory each morning before 6.25. Frequently he went on an inspection tour of our rooms. If a bed was unmade or a room not swept out, he left the door open. Sometimes he was far more accusatory in pointing out misdemeanours, as when on one occasion he asked one of my classmates: 'Mister, do you keep a cow in your room?'

I suspected that 'Cosie' considered that quite a number of us had no real vocations. In his weekly talks he frequently urged those who were thinking of leaving to do so as soon as possible. He implied that for them not to do so was unfair to those who would wish to have their places. Like the response to an antiphon he would add: 'Gentlemen. The gates of the college are always open.' He pushed this line to astonishing lengths. I recall one extraordinary stunt. In the penultimate talk before the Christmas holidays he gave a bleak account of a friend who had left the priesthood, while ministering in England. Then on the eve of the Christmas break he announced solemnly before night prayer: 'All those who do not intend to return after the holidays come to my room after night prayer.' On the first occasion we were in St Joseph's oratory after the holidays we were amazed to discover that we were all back to a man!

First theologians attended lectures in fundamental theology, moral theology, introduction to Sacred Scripture, the Old Testament, ecclesiastical history and canon law. In addition, they had classes in ascetic theology, Biblical Greek catechetics, history and geography of Palestine, pastoral theology and patrology. I also went to an optional class in German.

Rev Professor P. J. Hamell ('Joey') conducted the course on fundamental theology. He also lectured on patrology. A decent, kindly person, notwithstanding his best efforts, at his lectures students could be seen frequently looking at their watches. I recall re-checking mine on a number of occasions to see if it was going backwards! Although 'Joey' had a brilliant mind, his intelligence seemed to be intuitive rather than discursive. He constantly made assertions without any reference to the premises, whence they were derived. And, instead of lecturing to the 77 students in our class, he simply chatted as if to a single person.

In sharp contrast we had Rev Professor W. Conway ('Big Bill' because of his stature) for moral theology. He walked briskly into the lecture hall. At his first lecture he told us to listen and not to take notes, as he would dictate a summary towards the end of each session. A natural teacher, he exhibited remarkable clarity of mind and an obvious enthusiasm for his subject.

For introduction to Sacred Scripture, the exegesis of the New Testament and second year Hebrew we had Rev Professor J. O'Flynn ('Johno'). There were stories that 'Johno' was an insomniac. He was exceedingly shy and probably to compensate for this was never without a very stern expression and at times a wild stare, reminiscent of the gaze given by painters to Old Testament prophets. A consummate scholar, anything he did was carried out with great competence and seriousness.

Rev Professor M. J. Leahy ('Mickey Joe') had us for the Old Testament, history and geography of Palestine, Biblical Greek and first year Hebrew. Like Fr James Cosgrove it was clear that 'Mickey Joe' would have been far happier in a curacy in his diocese of Waterford and Lismore than filling the chair in Maynooth. However, because of ecclesiastical politics and his deference to his bishop, he found himself on the college staff. Most unassuming and likeable, he suffered from pathological shyness. This was exploited by the wiseacres who availed of every opportunity to embarrass him. I recall when we were studying the book of Jonah there was a rather facetious discussion about why the basic text of 'a big fish' was translated to mean a whale. As he preferred questions to be asked in this way, a note on the matter was sent up to 'Mickey Joe'. He opened it and without thinking read it out to the class: 'Would the big fish be a cod?' The resultant rowdyism took a few minutes to subside to the discomfort of many of us because of 'Mickey Joe's' manifest confusion.

Rev Professor P. J. Corish lectured on ecclesiastical history. For me he was the doyen of the professorial staff. I regard him as the finest teacher I was fortunate to have in all my educational experience. He pranced into the lecture hall and up the steps on to the rostrum or 'tub', as we called it. There followed a non-stop, all action lecture on some important aspect of the history of the church. Frequently he acted out extraordinary events such as the humiliation of the German emperor Henry IV by Pope Gregory VII at Canossa in 1077. Corish encouraged student reaction but sometimes received so much of it that he had difficulty in maintaining control. At such times his lively temperament added a further dimension of interest to his lectures. His impish sense of humour was unforgettable. I particularly enjoyed his double whammy at bishops and parish priests, when discussing the structure of the early Irish Church. The abbots of monasteries, not the bishops, exercised authority. He summed up the situation: 'The abbot kept a bishop the way a parish priest would keep a bull today.'

Rev Professor P. F. Cremin ('Frankie') lectured on canon law and moral theology. He was an excellent lecturer and generations of priests have been indebted to him for the carefully prepared, practical notes of his lectures on moral theology which he made available. Whatever he did, whether in the lecture hall or as chief celebrant at High Mass in the college chapel, he did with great competence and panache. Unfortunately his remarkable intelligence was not matched by much common sense. The two were in inverse proportion. 'Frankie' boasted about everything: his family, his county, his diocese, his remarkable academic achievements. He even boasted about his prowess as a footballer and hurler, always referring to himself as 'a dual player'. In class and outside it he made extensive use of the royal 'we'.

The students enjoyed him and the vast majority, including myself, had considerable affection for him, especially because of his child-like honesty. He was the favourite object of the mimics in every class. Some of 'Frankie's' peers found him difficult to take. Apart from his monumental lack of modesty, he was sternly conservative and never made a gesture in the direction of political correctness.

Rev Professor Kevin McNamara ('Kevin Mac') lectured on ascetical theology. He was clearly an outstanding scholar, was always well prepared and most earnest. But, because of the in-flexibility of his delivery, his lectures were soporific rather than interesting.

Rev Professor P. Birch took the second, third and fourth year theologians for one lecture a week in catechetics. He held the chair of education. His attitude to his lectures was extraordinary. Sometimes he arrived late which was quite unusual in Maynooth. And occasionally he would run out of material, spend the last fifteen minutes of the session gazing out the window of Loftus Hall at the orchard outside and fall into a deep reverie. Then, if he was aroused from this by the slightest noise from the students, he would become very upset!

Rev Professor J. G. McGarry ('Blades' because he occasionally arrived in class unshaven) took theologians once a week for pastoral theology. This involved elocution, preparing and delivering homilies and the study of sermons of some of the great preachers of the past, such as Bossuet, Fenelon, etc. He was extremely formal, always appeared wrapped up in his own thoughts, had a frosty expression, was never known to smile and when speaking to a student addressed him as if he was addressing an audience.

At the beginning of second theology, students had to make a number of choices. First they had to opt for either the seminarist/pass course or the university/honours course. In the event, generally-speaking, half of each class, some 40, would opt for the former. The other half of the class would then have to make a further decision: whether to follow the university course as such or in addition to prepare for the BD examination at the end of the third theology year. Here again the number would halve: some 20 opting for the former and another 20 for the latter. The relatively small number opting for the BD course was due to a number of factors. Two, however, were paramount: (1) the authorities insisted on maintaining a very high standard of achievement for success in the BD examination and (2), more daunting perhaps, all oral and written examinations for the degree had to be conducted in Latin!

In second, third and fourth theology we had Rev Professor G. Mitchell ('Mitch') for dogmatic theology, now generally referred to as systematic theology. He was a very good lecturer with a pleasant speaking voice. At the beginning of his lectures he made a sound like a snort. The wiseacres referred to this as 'Mitch strumming his catarrh'. And such was his fondness for the phrase 'At any rate' that some students took to counting the number of times he repeated it in a lecture. All I can recall after sitting at his feet for three years was a comment he made when he came to the end of Van Noort's tract on Penance. The last section concerned indulgences. With his usual snort he said: 'Gentlemen. All I want to say about this is I am certain indulgences won't do you any harm, but I am not sure if they can do you any good!'

Rev Professor J. McCarthy ('Ma Mac', because of some effeminate mannerisms) lectured on moral theology. A first-class performer, I vividly recall two wise comments he made at the beginning of the course. 'Gentlemen', he said, 'remember that in dealing with human nature anything that can happen will happen'. He also pointed out that from then onwards we would be mainly concerned with assessing the morality of human failure and weakness but that we should not forget that the essence of Christian morality was the two great commandments of love and their expression as articulated in the beatitudes.

Those of us following the BD course had extra lectures on canon law from Rev Professor J. Ahern. He was adequate, although at times, because of his very pronounced Cork accent, he could be almost unintelligible.

Rev Professor J. Newman lectured each week on sociology. He was very young-looking, handsome and there was an air of schoolboy innocence about him. Well-prepared and very earnest, his lectures were informative and interesting. Subsequently he was president of the college and later bishop of Limerick. In these taxing assignments he had only mixed success, which I believed was due mainly to the fact that he lacked the sliver of steel which unfortunately is required in the exercise of authority.

Rev Professor M. Harty, lectured on liturgy. A gentleman to his finger tips and a most gracious person, in manner he tended to be shy and tentative. His class was generally a rather relaxed affair between the more intensive sessions on theology. He was popular with our class and we chose him to be in our classpiece.

Two spiritual fathers resided in the college. I recall Fr Dan Costello, CM, and Fr James Doherty, CM. In intellectual terms Dan was a light-weight, James a heavy-weight. Both in their own way were equally effective. The former had responsibility for St Joseph's, the latter for St Mary's. They gave a conference/a spiritual talk to their charges once a week. Their role was to emphasise that all the varied activity in Maynooth was directed at preparing priests who would be totally dedicated to the spiritual service of the people in the parishes to which they would be assigned.

The academic life in Maynooth had a number of distinctive traditions. Three of those I found quite memorable. The first was the 'monthly call'. At the end of a month's lecturing the professor would name a day when he would examine on the material covered during the previous month. On the day his eyes would range up and down the class list and then he would call out the name and diocese of the examinee. If the student 'called' was not prepared this could be quite an ordeal. Often it was not made any easier when the professor would have invited the president, Mgr Edward J. Kissane, to attend. On these occasions the professor would be as eager to shine as the student. Should the latter lapse into English he would immediately be told: *'Latine, si vis'* ('Latin, if you please').

Mgr Kissane never spoke and sat sphinx-like throughout the exchanges between the professor and the students examined. For us students he was a remote figure. Although he was a distant relative, during my four years in the college I spoke to him on only two occasions. 'Kissane of Maynooth', as he was generally known, was most impressive in many ways, not least in his physical presence. Among the students there was a vague awareness of the high regard in which he was held by his peers inside and outside the college.

The tradition which most fascinated Dublin as well as Down and Conor students, also late arrivals in Maynooth after graduating from QUB, was what was known as 'gallery'. This was student reaction to the professors. It took the form of stamping on the floor, hissing and above all 'shushing' which sometimes reached an amazing crescendo. Nearly all the professors allowed this, something which was never tolerated at Clonliffe or UCD. Significantly the two professors who were most tolerant of it were the two outstanding lecturers in the college: Corish and 'Frankie'. Each in his own way managed it as masterfully as Sir John Barbarolli handled the rowdy crowd at the last night of the proms. Corish would pretend he was on the verge of losing his temper. 'Frankie' would affect to be wearied by such a display of immaturity.

The third tradition was the 'free class' which the professor was obliged to give at the end of each term. For me 'Mitch' and 'Frankie' were the two stars of this practice. 'Mitch' was a fan of the American humorist, Alfred Damon Runyon, whose stories about New York night-life were collected in *Guys and dolls* (New York 1931). Obviously enjoying himself, 'Mitch' would read a selection of these stories to us superbly.

'Frankie' had no peer in this aspect of the academic life! He came into class and invited the students to suggest any topic on which they wished him to speak. Generally, among other subjects, he would be asked to comment on the world situation. *Ex Tempore*, or at least seemingly so, he would give a masterly exposition on it. Towards the end of the class the students would request a song. For about seven or eight minutes he would resist this, in spite of enormous 'gallery'. Then out from under his toga he would produce a tuning fork, strike a note and give a beautiful rendering of 'The castle of Dromore' – in the vernacular of course! The irritatingly long seven or eight minutes of coaxing would be more than compensated for by the wonderful smile of pleasure with which he acknowledged the thunderous applause for his effort.

In Maynooth sport flourished as much as the academic life. There were facilities for croquet, handball, swimming and tennis. At the annual Easter sports day all the track and field events were keenly contested. An inter-diocesan soccer league was organised, with Armagh and Derry usually reaching the finals. But the sporting events which attracted most attention were the inter-class matches in Gaelic football and hurling, played each Wednesday and Saturday in the 'high field'.

Of the five class football teams in senior house, ours won the inter-class competition in their BA year and we were runners-up in the following four years. Those featuring in class teams were college and/or county players. Our key players were T. J. McGuinness who featured at centre-half-back as he had for the Ulster colleges, Jack Mahon of Galway and Jim Aiken of Armagh (later the well-known entertainments promoter) at centre-field and Christy McGrath of Carlow at centre-half-forward. Our class hurling team lost a number of its best players after the BA year and was the weakest in the league. However, we occasionally enjoyed surprising some of the more fancied sides.

Such was the intensity of the inter-class matches, especially those in hurling, that frequently players would have to report to Sister Louise. Widowed twice before joining the Daughters of

Charity of St Vincent de Paul, she presided over the senior infirmary (the 'List'). A story went the rounds among the students that
the only way to get into the senior infirmary was either in an
ambulance or on a stretcher. Her unfailing response to any ailment
or sign of ill-health was to present the patient with three tiny
white tablets. When I called on her with the flu I was given these
and on another occasion when I arrived to have a cut dressed
after a particularly competitive inter-class hurling match I received the same treatment! In sharp contrast was Sister Enda.
Also a Daughter of Charity, she was in charge of the infirmary in
Clonliffe. She had an excess of sympathy for the students and in
the cold and harsh weather sometimes as many as a fifth of them
with her permission would skip the early part of the daily programme and simply arrive down for breakfast to the obvious
annoyance of the dean, Fr Cathal McCarthy.

The *Aula Maxima* (great hall) was mainly used for recreation
and entertainment. It was managed by a students' committee
and here the various drama societies presented plays in Irish
and English, generally produced by the distinguished actor, Ray
MacAnally, a former student of the college. However, the highlight of the dramatic season was the 'Old Fourths'. This was a
'musical' presented by the fourth year theologians in which each
of them had a part! The producer of our 'Old Fourths' was Pat
Aherne, later the genius behind and director of *Siamsa Tíre*.
Films were also screened on free days, including the eves of the
break-up of the college before the Christmas and summer
holidays. But on such occasions the films did not attract much
attention, and there would be general mayhem, owing to the
high-spirits of all at the ending of examinations and the prospect
of 'imminent freedom'.

The functions in the *Aula Maxima* were held during periods
of recess: All Saints Day, Shrove, St Patrick's Day and especially
the Easter holidays when we remained in the college. During
Easter, the senior dean, Rev Dr Gerard Montague ('Monty') en-
deavoured to provide us with first-class entertainment, generally
of the high-culture variety. He invariably had the National

Symphony Orchestra give a concert. And, if any well-known
touring musicians or opera singer were in Dublin, he would
invite them to present their programme in Maynooth. 'Monty'
would also call on the service of distinguished lecturers.

I always regarded the senior college library as something of
an anomaly. I never sat down to read a book in it nor, as far as I
can recall, did any of my fellow-students. A notice near the
entrance read:

Whoever takes a book out of this library
incurs excommunication
ipso facto

I regarded this as much a curiosity as the 'haunted room'. In fact, I
resented it, considering that it was stretching the jurisdiction of the
internal forum one book too far! The college museum, established
in 1934, was small but interesting. It will always be associated with
the two visits the ill-fated Austrian Empress Elizabeth paid to the
college and the early experiments in electricity conducted by Rev
Professor Nicholas Callan.

There was never much room for emotion in Maynooth. But I
confess that I unfailingly became misty-eyed during one of the
college customs. This was on the Sundays of Advent, when the
almost 400 students in the cavernous senior refectory stood after
dinner and solemnly sang two verses of the *Adeste Fideles*.

The most interesting feature of the college for me was the
diversity of the student body. The students were from parishes
which extended from Malin Head to Mizen Head. In subsequent
years when hearing an Irish accent I have been generally able to
place it by identifying it with that of a fellow-student in
Maynooth. The college also had a sprinkling of expatriates.

Bonding among the students took place at a number of levels.
Class consciousness developed from praying and attending
classes and lectures together. It was also promoted by a class
debating and other societies. Most of all it was nurtured by
identifying with the class football and hurling teams.

Because of the spaciousness of the college before the end of
recreational periods students of the various dioceses congregated

at their own specific area or 'Pos'. Thereby one also became close to co-diocesans. But the closest friendships were forged with those with whom one sat at table for four meals each day.

In the senior refectory students were seated at tables for ten. My 'immediates' (those next to me) were Tom Marsh of Waterford and Lismore and Paddy Marron of Clogher. I became a life-long friend of both. We were the tail-end of the class and so at our table also were Tom Murphy of Ardagh, senior of the next class, and Matt O'Donnell of Galway. Matt had been in our class but had stayed back a year to complete an MA.

Tom Marsh was what Canon Patrick Sheehan called the 'First of firsts' – he was first in the final examination for the BD. Subsequently he completed a doctorate in Dunboyne House, taught for a few years in St John's College, Waterford, and thereafter until his death was professor of dogmatic theology in Maynooth. I greatly regretted missing Tom's obsequies. I was on holiday on the continent and, despite his best efforts, Paddy Marron was not able to contact me. When I returned home I paid a prayerful and sad visit to his grave in the memory-laden cemetery in the college.

Tom Marsh and Matt O'Donnell, who subsequently held the chair of metaphysics and was later president, were devoid of small-talk and spent a lot of time in deep reflection. Another brilliant classmate, Tom Finan, who spent his life in the college as professor of ancient classics, was even more silent than Tom or Matt. There was a story among his peers that Tom Finan spoke only to God! Tom Marsh and Matt O'Donnell differed in that Tom was always eager to discuss matters dealt with in class, whereas this was off-limits as far as Matt was concerned.

By the time the 67 of us were ordained in 1957 we were acutely aware of the high standards which would be expected of us. Almost sixty years earlier Canon Sheehan, in emphasising how uncompromising in the cause of right and independent of threat or patronage Maynooth men were, wrote:

> Then came Maynooth, which founded on government subsidies, poured forth from its gates the strongest, fiercest,

most fearless army of priests that ever fought for the spiritual
and temporal interests of the people - men of large physique
and iron constitutions, who spent ten hours a day on horse-
back, despised French claret, loved their people and chast-
ised them like fathers, but were prepared to defend them
with their lives and the outpouring of their blood against
their hereditary enemies. Intense in their faith, of stainless
lives and spotless reputations, their words cut like razors;
but they had the hearts of mothers for the little ones of their
flocks.

Even in 1957 we considered Sheehan to be indulging in a little
hyperbole. However, as we left Maynooth, we were in no doubt
about our duty to God, the church and our country and that our
success would be measured according to the service we rendered to the people entrusted to our care.

CHAPTER 3

Presentation College, Bray
1957-1960

At the beginning of September 1957 I received my first appoint-
ment in the archdiocese of Dublin. I was appointed chaplain to
Presentation College, Bray, a priest-teacher in Bray Vocational
School and was directed to enroll in the Higher Diploma in
Education course in University College, Dublin, for the academic
year 1957-8.

Presentation College, Bray, was established by the Presentation
Brothers in 1924. In 1957 it had over 70 boarders and about 130
day-boys. My basic duties as chaplain consisted of 7.30 am Mass
Monday to Friday for the Brothers and senior boarders, Mass for
all at 10 am on Saturday and Sunday, an hour's session for
Confessions on Saturday evening and a conference (a 25 minute
talk) to the boarders every Sunday at noon. For this I received
£250 per annum and my breakfast each morning.

During my three year association with the College I developed an admiration for the small community of dedicated and
selfless brothers who, with an even smaller lay-staff, ran a very
successful second-level school. However my general attitude to
the College was somewhat ambivalent. This reflected my attitude
to Bray. I noted and regarded it as unfair that the greater Dublin
area, including Bray, seemed to have a higher standard of living
than the rest of the country, in terms of employment, educational
opportunities and wage levels. Also in Bray there was a noticeable degree of snobbery and an emphasis on class. Coming from
Listowel, where this was almost non-existent, except for a handful of out-of-town bank officials and a few others, this grated on
me. But most of all I was confirmed in the prejudice I brought to
the place as being part of the 'Pale'. There was a perceptible

Anglophile/Anti-Irish atmosphere which I did not find congenial.

One incident left me in no doubt that such a cocktail of attitudes was prevalent in the College. Apart from a PT class, there were no other facilities for games in Bray Vocational School. I organised a Gaelic football team. The catchment area of the school was North Wicklow so many of the youngsters came from districts where Gaelic football was played. I arranged a few matches with St Brendan's Christian Brothers School, then just being established on the outskirts of the town. Nearly all the boarders in Presentation College were from Gaelic football areas so I arranged a match between them and the team from the Vocational School in the College. The Brothers were quite pleased with the idea. It was successful and we had a return match. I might add that these matches were played at a time when the Rugby season in the College had ended, with the almost yearly first-round exit of the College's senior and junior teams from the Leinster Cup.

After the second Gaelic football match there were ructions. A procession of parents threatened the Brother Superior that if another Gaelic football match was played in the College they would transfer their boys elsewhere. Ostensibly the parents were objecting to Gaelic football but, as most people suspected, their major concern was that it was being played by youngsters of working-class parents from the poorer parts of the Bray district and they did not wish them to be mixing with the pupils of the College. Ironically the most vociferous of those parents were among those least supportive of the College. Brother Columba, the bursar, often complained to me how, despite repeated requests, it was well-nigh impossible to get them to pay the modest College fees. This was true even of the College's most distinguished *alumni*. I urged him on a number of occasions that in fairness to the other fee-paying parents he should insist that all such parents who were ostentatiously well-off should be compelled to pay the fees. But he always demurred, claiming it would cause too much of a scandal and furore.

As a priest-teacher in Bray Vocational School I had two sessions a week in Religious Knowledge for the Junior Technical Boys, Junior Engineers, Senior Engineers, Junior Commerce and Intermediate Commerce classes. The other priest-teacher, my class-mate, Fr Leo Quinlan, chaplain of St Gerard's, Bray, also had ten hours teaching a week in the Vocational School. The introduction of priest-teachers into the Vocational Schools under the aegis of the Dublin Vocational Educational Committee proved very satisfactory to all concerned. The priest-teachers were supervised by Fr Frank McCabe who acted as a kind of inspector. We were provided with a textbook which had been prepared by Fr Fergal McGrath, SJ, the distinguished educationalist and scholar. His *Life in Christ*, Parts I, II and III, was comprehensive with each part to be taught in each succeeding year. It was very useful as a teacher's manual and, while rather advanced for many of my pupils, it was amply illustrated and I had them all get a copy of it.

The educational standard of many of my pupils was not high and quite a few were less than average in intelligence. Because I was the junior teacher in the school which was over-crowded I had to take some classes in the woodwork room and the assembly hall. All my life when teaching I have never sat down. I remain standing or walk about so as to engage the entire class and ensure that everyone is actively involved. I have never forgotten the exemplary teaching style of Bryan MacMahon in this regard. As I had to speak in a loud voice in the assembly hall and woodwork room and try to make a difficult subject intelligible to not very receptive classes, I sometimes found two such consecutive teaching periods physically quite taxing. In retrospect I regard this experience of teaching religion in the Vocational School for three years as having been an excellent training in communication.

John Meagher, the principal, was a strict disciplinarian. I was also very strict, repeating the kind of regime I had experienced as a pupil. Without exception, the youngsters were very pleasant. In addition, the members of the staff were very kind and

supportive to Leo and myself. This was especially true of Paddy
O'Riordan, one of the commerce teachers. Paddy, a native of
Rathvilly, was very able, gentle, quiet, a Gaelic football enthusiast,
having played for his county, and the most popular teacher,
both among his peers and the pupils. Conversely Roddy
Connolly, son of the Easter 1916 leader, was quite unpopular.
When he entered the staff-room only Leo and I attempted to engage him in conversation. He was mainly responsible for this
situation, having a supercilious and 'do you know who I am'
attitude which was sometimes quite insufferable. That having
been said, he was a fine teacher of commerce. Another unusual
member of the staff was Yann Renard-Goulet who had a few
classes a week. An artist and sculptor of repute, he was a Breton
nationalist who was accused of collaborating with the Germans
in the early 1940s and had a death sentence passed on him after
World War II. Bearded and sometimes with a large wide-
brimmed hat, he darted furtively in and out of the staff room.

Both the principal and the staff were most supportive when
each year I organised a three-day retreat. Fr Paul Leonard, SJ,
conducted it on the first two years and I was impressed by his
attempts to try out the liturgical reforms of the Mass then being
tentatively proposed by Fr Clifford Howell, SJ, the aim of which
was to encourage greater participation by those attending Mass.
The annual school outing and staff dinners were most enjoyable.
I regret to recall that some twenty years after I had left Bray it
came to my attention that two of my former pupils, whom I
remembered as being well below average intelligence, had been
arraigned for murder following a brawl with visitors from
Scotland. The payment I received for my teaching in Bray
Vocational School was not princely. From archbishop's house I
received £66 for my first year and £150 in each of the following
two years.

In October Leo and I enrolled, as directed, in the Higher
Diploma in Education course at UCD. Fr Seán Ó Catháin, SJ, was
lecturer in education and, although not a professor, the head of
the department. He was a very shy person, always seemed to
have his eyes downcast, and had a rather pawky manner and

sense of humour. However, even though there were over 170 taking his course he had no problem in maintaining discipline. He gave two lectures a week on the 'Principles of Education' and two on the 'History of Education'. And each week he had John McKenna lecture on 'Educational Psychology', Fr Bertie Crowe on 'Ethics' and a number of others dealt with 'Teaching Methods' and 'Teaching Practice'. Leo and I came in from Bray four days a week for the lectures which ran from 4 to 5 and 5 to 6. In addition to lectures and teaching practice those taking the course had to write a major essay. Ó Catháin assessed these and then had a discussion with each student. Besides marking his own papers at the end of the year he was on the board which conducted an oral examination of each student. By the end of the year I had formed a high opinion of him on account of the manner in which he committed himself to his work.

I commuted between Bray and Earlsfort Terrace on a scooter. After being soaked to the skin on many occasions throughout January I went down with pleurisy at the beginning of February. A positive memory from this was the camaraderie of Fr Tom Butler, SM, with whom I shared a room in the Bon Secours Hospital, Glasnevin, for over two weeks. A negative one was the ill-informed comments of two of my classmates who were then chaplains to TB hospitals and who declared that because of my condition I would be in hospital for at least three months! After being released from hospital I went home to Listowel to convalesce for about three weeks. I was concerned at missing so much of the second term at UCD but in the end it worked out alright and I managed a second class honours, Grade I. While I was at home I told my uncle about 'all I had to do'. He listened patiently and then asked me to tot up in hours my weekly commitment which I did. His reply to this was: 'Sonny boy, remember all the persons you will be expected to serve for the rest of your life will have at least forty hours work a week and that very often very disagreeable work.' I have never since complained of being too busy!

Besides my principal duties I had a number of extra-curricular commitments. A few years previously Fr Tom Feehily had

succeeded Fr Jim Kavanagh as director of the Dublin Institute of
Catholic Sociology. Tom was in an expansionist mood and set
up centres around the diocese in addition to the main centre at
Eccles Street. He asked me to run a centre in Bray and I agreed.
The Institute took care of the organisation and administration of
the centre. My input was a session every Friday evening from 8
to 10 at the Vocational School. I would lecture for three quarters
of an hour, there would be a cup of tea and finally an open discussion. I ran the centre for the three years I was in Bray. In the
first year we did a course on sociology based on Fr Jim
Kavanagh's *Manual of social ethics;* in the second year we studied
all aspects of Communism; and in the third I attempted a more
advanced treatment of ethics with reference to contemporary
philosophy. I managed to keep all eighteen of my students over
the three years. They were an interesting group: two medical
doctors, a solicitor, the principal of the national school, a
number of civil servants and the genius of the class, Michael
Ledwidge. Michael was a native of Bray and had left school at
fourteen years of age. At my persuasion, even while he was still
attending my sociology class, he enrolled at either Bolton Street
or Kevin Street Technology College and achieved a qualification
in civil engineering.

I might add that Fr Liam Breen was chairman of the Board of
Management of the D.I.C.S. and showed his appreciation of my
running the Bray centre by inviting Leo Quinlan and myself to a
most enjoyable lunch with him and Fr Michael Clarke every
Saturday. They shared a house on the Old Connaught Road and
had responsibility for the district around St Peter's in Little Bray,
then a chapel of ease to Holy Redeemer parish in Bray. Because
of the generation gap there was considerable sparring between
both Leo and me and the senior men. This sometimes became
rather heated and on a few occasions after Leo, who is even
more outspoken than I am, made a few outrageously abrasive
remarks I thought our enjoyable Saturday interlude would end.
But Liam and Michael proved to be more tolerant than I had
given them credit for.

I was glad to celebrate Mass, hear Confessions and to preach occasionally in the two parishes in Bray, not least because the priests were particularly generous when I helped in this way. This generally occurred when someone was away on holiday. Holy Redeemer parish was by far the busiest of the two parishes so I had more contact with their staff. Monsignor John Fitzpatrick was the parish priest. The two senior men, Frs Breen and Clarke, had responsibility for St Peter's district and Frs Jack Baker, Donal McDowell and Fred Hayes served the rest of the parish. 'Fitz', as he was known among the priests, used Baker as a kind of adjutant. Baker was ideal for the role. A martinet, he was meticulous about his appearance and ensured that anything he attempted went like clock-work. He hired me to hear Confessions every Saturday night from 7 to 9.30. After the session I adjourned to his room for television and supper. I found Jack Baker very likeable, although he was not as popular as the other staff members, owing to his abrupt manner.

My favourite priest in Bray was 'Fitz'. Like his brother Willie he had been expelled from St Kieran's College for smoking. They transferred to Clonliffe and Ossory's loss was Dublin's gain. Willie served for many years with distinction in the Killester-Raheny area and chaired a number of important diocesan committees. But he is best remembered today as the founder of St Vincent's football and hurling club. The brothers came from farming stock from Mountmellick and this remained evident in everything about them.

The Bray 'Fitz' had been a well-known theologian in his early years and in the 1920s and 1930s had contributed in the theological journals to discussions on the crucial issues of that time, not least the morality of hunger-striking and the question of what constituted legitimate secular authority. Apart from being parish priest of Bray, 'Fitz' chaired a number of important educational committees. I took to 'Fitz' from the first time I met him. He was a simple man and devoid of affectation of any kind. We had frequent chats during the ten minute break at the Saturday night Confessions. On one occasion he confided to me that the handful of priests who tended to be obsessive about liturgy were somehow lacking in manliness. I was not surprised when his reaction to the new Easter Vigil ceremonies was to announce that instead of presiding at them he would be retiring an hour earlier that night!

'Fitz' was a marvellous preacher. On one occasion I was waiting in the sacristy to assist at the distribution of Holy Communion and when he came in after preaching I complimented him on a few purple patches, including the expression 'lice on the body-politic'. In his sermon he had included a lash at vandals who had done a great deal of destruction in the grounds of the convent at Ravenswell, and whom he had referred to in these terms. I said unthinkingly that the expression was Churchillian. He immediately told me that he had come across it during the week when reading one of Churchill's volumes on *The history of the English-speaking peoples*.

'Fitz' was ungainly in his movements and managed to be so even when distributing Holy Communion. While he had a deep and reverential respect for the Real Presence, he was almost oblivious to the importance of physical decorum. I recall helping with the heavy communions one Christmas morning. Despite his age, 'Fitz' attended all the Masses from the earliest onwards. At the 11 o'clock Mass a large, stray dog wandered into the sanctuary and began to follow him along the rails as he distributed Communion. Instead of stopping and calling on the sacristan to deal with the dog he continued to distribute Communion while at the same time drawing a kick at the dog! An even more amusing aspect of this incident was the obvious utter dismay of Jack Baker as he observed the performance.

A refreshing aspect of 'Fitz' was that he cared little of what people thought of him. Once he complained to his housekeeper that he found the light coming into his car blinding on very bright days. She then had, without his knowledge, curtains fitted to all the windows, except the windscreen. Despite the critical comments of parishioners about the unusual decor of the parish priest's car, he had not the heart to tell the housekeeper to have the curtains taken down again.

My most enduring memory of 'Fitz' was his reaction to an incident which occurred during a planned-giving campaign in the parish. Wells, a Church of England consultancy organisation, had been invited into the archdiocese to improve collections and fund-raising in parishes. A major part of the scheme was to invite representatives of the families of the parish to a dinner and appeal to them to pledge a reasonable contribution, relative to their means, to parish needs. The person to make the pitch was carefully chosen. He had to be both highly-regarded and popular.

In Bray it was not difficult to make the choice. Brendan Donnelly was the most popular person in the parish and with good reason. He was both exceedingly wealthy and generous. Although he had qualified as a medical doctor – it seems after about eleven years – he did not spend much time practising his profession. At the time of the planned-giving campaign he was canvassing to be the next captain of Woodbrook Golf Club. Accordingly for the gala dinner two large marquees were erected at Woodbrook.

In preparation for his address to the great and good of the parish Brendan was briefed by the Wells consultant. It so happened that during the previous week Brendan had spoken at a Stag party at the golf club. Word filtered out that he had 'brought the house down'! On the day of the parish dinner Brendan was quite nervous and began to imbibe during the day. The result was that when he stood up to speak that evening he swayed quite perceptibly and for a few moments seemed to have a blackout. Then he brightened up and said: 'Rt Rev Mgr, Rev Fathers, Sisters, Ladies and Gentlemen, Standing here to-night I feel like King David when he was presented with his one hundred concubines. I know what is expected of me but I do not know where to begin!'

After that inauspicious beginning Brendan did not make much of a recovery. Although furious, 'Fitz' remained sphinx-like. I did not recall anybody daring to ask him what he thought of Brendan's performance. In retrospect I believe that this little *contre temps* was most useful. It helped to dispel a fair bit of tension which had arisen owing to a surprisingly large number of well-to-do and rich people being quite hurt when asked to make a reasonable contribution to the running expenses of the parish.

The Legion of Mary was very active in Bray at that time. They had established their centre 'Fatima House' opposite the International Hotel. This was used for meetings of the various *praesidia*. They also had added a good-sized hall between the house and the railway-line behind it. Leo Quinlan and I were spiritual directors of a number of praesidia. We also helped with teenage socials organised by the Legion at Fatima House every Sunday night. These were run from 7.30 to 11 and involved disco dancing with two interludes: one for the recitation of the Rosary and another for a cup of tea and biscuits. I was most impressed by the wonderful example and leadership given by the Legion of Mary boys and girls to the teenagers of the district. Liam Cleere, Vincent O'Connell and Michael Woods were outstanding in this regard. Liam Cleere and Michael Woods even at that early stage were showing evidence of remarkable ability and in the case of Woods single-minded ambition. Liam Ó Maolchatha and Mícheál Ó Fearghail were leading members of an Irish-speaking *presidium*. Their *Réalt* group eventually succeeded in setting up the *Scoil Lán-Ghaelach* in the town.

Frank Duff, the co-founder and outstanding protagonist of the Legion of Mary, addressed a number of large gatherings at Fatima House. At that time he was almost deaf, spoke at length in a dreary monotone and was not very prepossessing in appearance. There was no doubting his sincerity. I was impressed by the deep respect the young members of the Legion of Mary had for him. But I could never find him other than rather tetchy and tiresome.

During my time in Bray I had accommodation with the Corcoran family, who resided opposite the entrance to Presentation College. It was a large family: a granny, father, mother, four daughters and four sons, with three daughters elsewhere. At the request of the Presentation Brothers the family had agreed to provide 'digs' for the chaplain. They agreed to take me on the same terms as my predecessor, Fr John J. Greehy who had been sent to do post-graduate studies in Rome. I had my meals with the family. This was a new experience for me, having been raised as an only child. I found all the family very friendly and helpful.

Paddy Corcoran, the father, was a 'Redmondite' from Waterford city. A member of the head office staff of Texaco Ireland, he spoke in a low voice and with a slightly Anglicised accent. He loved amateur dramatics and was an excellent actor. A thorough gentleman, he was one of the most patient and toler-ant men I have ever met. Two fond remembrances of my time with the family stand out. The first was the occasional Sunday afternoon drives in the summer to the beauty spots of County Wicklow and the second was attending on Saturday afternoons in the winter the home and away matches of Greystones Rugby team, on which one of the Corcoran boys was one of the more skilful players. Paddy Corcoran always insisted on me accom-panying him on these enjoyable excursions.

At the end of my second year in Bray Leo Quinlan was appointed as a secretary in archbishop's house. Later he was sent to the Teutonic College in Rome to study canon law. I envied him, as at that time I would have been thrilled to have had the opportunity of post-graduate studies in Rome or indeed any-where else. Leo was replaced in St Gerard's by Fr Joe Hogan. I continued with him the close partnership I had with Leo and we met for lunch each week in that regard.

During my second summer at Bray I had an interesting interlude helping out for a month in the parish of Bonnyrigg, near Edinburgh. The parish priest, Fr Joe MacArdle, had a heart attack and the Passionist priest, Fr Leo Marron, who normally supplied for him was on holiday. Fr Joe's brother, Kevin, was the master of St Mary's hospital in the Phoenix Park. He contacted me on the recommendation of the chaplain and asked me to stand in for his brother. I agreed.

That evening I travelled to Turnhouse airport and was collected by a parishioner. There was a resident housekeeper and I was given the use of Fr Joe's car. My basic duties involved a 6.45 am Mass in Nazareth House, a home for elderly people run by Sisters, an hour's Confessions on Saturday evening and two Masses on Sunday. The parishioners were very upbeat. They had just completed their new church. It was a dual-purpose building: on weekdays it was a small partitioned-off oratory *cum* community hall and on Sunday the whole building was used as a church.

Almost all the parishioners were coal miners and their families. I noticed that the men were all low in stature and when walking and standing tended to lean forward. A few of them asked me if I would like to see where they worked. I jumped at the opportunity to do so. It took a half-hour to get from the surface to the coal face: down a half mile in the cage and then crouching in a small wagon to the end of the track. The heat and dust at the coal face were far worse than I had anticipated. Apart from the area where the cage landed, I was not able to stand up straight during my entire visit to the mine.

On returning to the surface I decided to visit all the sick miners in the parish each week. Those who were not too ill were at home and I called on them on weekdays. The most seriously ill were in the Royal Infirmary in Edinburgh. These I visited on the three Sunday afternoons. There were eleven suffering from an advanced stage of silicosis. It was my first experience of this most distressing condition. Until his heart gives out the sufferer is constantly struggling to breathe like a person who is slowly drowning. All the fatally ill miners were under forty years of age. The wing where those suffering from this condition were cared for was some distance from the main hospital to ensure that other patients were not disturbed by the constant coughing, wheezing and occasional moaning emanating from it.

In Bonnyrigg I had my first and thankfully last personal experience of overt anti-Catholic bigotry. One morning as the housekeeper and myself had arrived back from Nazareth House after Mass and were about to enter the presbytery I noticed that she had got visibly upset. I looked across the street where a milkman in his mid-twenties was standing with his tongue stuck out at me. After the initial shock of amazement I began to laugh and pointed at him. This caused him to become apoplectic. I was lucky there were no stones lying about as I am sure he would have thrown them at me.

During my first week in Bonnyrigg I learned that another Irish priest, Fr Brian Magee, CM, was doing supply work at Rosewell, just five miles away. I called on him and together we had many enjoyable outings, including trips to Loch Lomond, the Trossachs and the Vincentian House in Lanark.

By my third year in Bray I was beginning to feel under-employed. I read widely and in the evenings spent a lot of time looking at TV with one or other of the curates in the Queen of Peace parish from whom I had an invitation to visit anytime.

I also visited Jim Lyons and his charming wife, Maura, quite a lot. Jim had called on me almost as soon as I had arrived in Bray. He was secretary of Bray Emmets Gaelic Football Club and constantly on the lookout for players for his senior team. I played at full-back on the team for three years and was able to get my friends Frs Gabriel Colleran and Eamon McSweeney to play also. The team generally consisted of three priests, six members from the local Garda station and six natives of Bray! In the first two years we got only beyond the first match in the Wicklow County Championship but in the third we reached the semi-final, losing out to St. Patrick's, Wicklow, who at that time were the county champions year after year.

The support for Gaelic games in Bray was minimal. Nearly all of those with any interest in them were from out of town. Typical was the effervescent and popular Matt Britain, the grand old man of Bray Emmets. Although in his early nineties, he looked like a man in his forties, and had won All-Ireland football medals with his native Wexford at the beginning of the century.

During my final year in Bray and two and a half years in Cabra West I was a member of the Dublin diocesan soccer team. The team had been organised about twenty years earlier by Frs Brian Kelly and Jack McCarthy. During the season we managed to play a match every two or three weeks. We played teams in the various major seminaries but not exclusively. I recall playing teams representing the staff in Grangegorman Hospital, the garrison in Cathal Brugha barracks and other such institutions. The pick of the teams we played were the Jesuits in Milltown Park and the students in St Columban's, Dalgan Park, Navan. The team enjoyed particularly our trips to St Columban's Dalgan Park, and St Patrick's, Kiltegan. After the match we would join the college staff for a splendid meal and a sing-song afterwards.

Fr Michael Cleary and a few others tried to organise a Dublin diocesan Gaelic football team. However it proved very difficult to turn out fifteen players for matches and the attempt had to be abandoned. I recall playing only two matches: one with Mick's own home club: St Bridgid's, in Blanchardstown: and the other with the priests and students of some Religious Order in O'Toole park.

By the summer of 1960 I was not finding Bray much of a challenge any more and I was looking forward to the change which, after three years, I knew was imminent.

CHAPTER 4

Most Precious Blood, Cabra West
1960-1962

In the summer of 1960 I found my name on the 'Honours List'. This is how my colleagues referred to the annual list of transfers issued in June each year. I had been appointed a reader in the parish of the Most Precious Blood, Cabra West This working-class parish of 16,000 had been constituted from the Cabra and Aughrim Street parishes in 1946 and a large, modern church had recently been completed to replace a temporary chapel which had been in use until then. At that time the most junior curate in many of the larger parishes was a reader. In my case this meant that, while the other curates in the parish had a salary of £21 a week, I received £6 and the balance due to me was each month allocated to the parish debt account. I was to replace Fr Pat Russell, who had been on loan from the archdiocese of Cashel and was going to Yale to take up a studentship in German language and literature.

My new parish priest was Canon Val Burke. He was a simple, pious and saintly man. In his early years he had ministered in parishes in the 'Liberties', where he was greatly loved by the poor. He was known as 'Toucher' Burke because he was forever raising funds for charitable or pious purposes. He was single-minded in his commitment to the well-being of his parishioners. I recall him weeping when none of the children in the sixth class of St Finbar's Boys National School passed the Primary Certificate. He feared that this meant that these boys would eventually be trapped in dead-end jobs for the rest of their lives. He was much more upset than most of the parents! His love for the parishioners was reciprocated and, when he died, they insisted that he be buried among them, next to the church he had helped to build.

The two senior curates: Fr Pat Farrell and Fr Steve Greene, shared a house on the Cabra Road just outside the parish. Fr Farrell was rather highly-strung, keen on the out of doors, seemed to be impervious to cold weather never wearing an overcoat, and was followed everywhere by a large dog. He was also an avid reader, a keen bridge player and often relaxed by playing patience.

Apart from his basic duties, he specialised in running a most successful 'Children's Mass'. Such were the crowds attending Mass on each Sunday morning, that Masses were celebrated every half hour from seven to noon. This meant Masses lasting twenty to twenty-five minutes. Almost simultaneously, one priest would celebrate, another would distribute Holy Communion and a third would preach a five to seven minute sermon. However, an exception was made for the 'Children's Mass' which was from 10 to 10.45. Pat, who was a very shy person, seemed to lose all inhibitions when conducting the 'Children's Mass'. The large church would be packed, two-thirds of it by children and the rest by parents and adults. Pat acted rather than told the lives of saints or stories from the Bible from little books published by the Salesians of Don Bosco. He would always end in such a way that the children would be hooked and would come the next Sunday for 'Fr Farrell's follier-upper'. The children's reaction was like that at a pantomime. Heroes and heroines were cheered and villains were booed.

Pat was not as effective in preaching to adults largely because of his bellowing voice, nor was I very effective especially during my first year in Cabra West I carefully wrote out my sermons but learned by experience that a piece of good speaking was different from a piece of good writing, that the only sure way of engaging a congregation was by looking at them and speaking to them as if one to one. Thereafter I never wrote sermons or even sermon notes.

Fr Steve Greene was Napoleonic in stature and manner. Of outstanding ability, he was a superb organiser. Each year he organised the *Corpus Christi* procession and ensured that practically

every person in the parish took part in it and that not only every
road but almost every home was appropriately beflagged and
decorated for the occasion. He conducted the Women's Sacred
Heart Sodality, organised the various collections and fund-raising in the parish, was chaplain to the Boy Scouts and managed
St Finbar's Parish Hall. And he did everything with an enviable
competence and thoroughness.

I shared a presbytery with Fr Cecil Johnston and his housekeeper, Mrs Rita Johnson. The similarity of the surnames occasionally caused a wry smile among parishioners. Mrs Johnson
had been left a young widow and she had no family. Both she
and Cecil contributed to my stay in the parish being a very
happy one. Mrs Johnson, a gentle lady of great charm, spoiled
Cecil and myself as the sons she never had.

Cecil and I were the junior staff members and so, as was
customary, we were given the toughest assignments: the poor
and the youth. Apart from running the Men's Sodality, Cecil
was chaplain to the parish's two St Vincent de Paul Conferences
and was manager of St Finbar's National School.

I had the same basic duties as the other curates: daily and
Sunday Masses, Saturday confessions, preaching, monthly pro-
vision of the sacraments for the elderly and ill in their homes
(First Friday calls) and conducting baptisms, marriages and
funerals for those in a district of between 4,000 and 5,000 people.
In addition, I had responsibility for the Teenage Sodality, St
Finbar's Boys Club, the altar boys, chaplaincy to St Declan's
Christian Brothers School, the Legion of Mary and the 'Poor
Box'. Like the Men's and Women's Sodalities, the Teenage
Sodality met each month on a Friday evening with a general
communion on the following Sunday. As with the other activities
in the parish, there were selfless and committed parishioners
who helped with this devotional exercise. Through their efforts
and those of about thirty splendid youngsters, who acted as prefects, I was able to have some 450 boys and girls aged 15 to 18, at
a rosary, sermon and Benediction on a Friday evening each
month, with a general communion for them on the following

Sunday morning. The majority of these youngsters would have finished school and have jobs in shops or factories in the city. Having to rise in winter and summer before 7 o'clock each day and spend the day at work ensured that within a very short time they were as mature as any adult can be.

Notwithstanding the efforts of the men who helped to run it, St Finbar's Boys Club was not a great success. We provided gymnastics, boxing lessons and elementary woodwork. However, the less 'wild youngsters' joined the boy-scouts and we in the Boys Club were left with the most intractable ones. Most of the time all we managed to do was to simply divert them from mindless vandalism.

At the weekly meeting of the forty to fifty altar-boys, for the most part I had the youngsters teach each other how to serve Mass. This took some time, as the responses were then in Latin. However their enthusiasm was infectious. It was my job to ensure that the five priests in the parish had a pair of servers at their daily and Sunday Masses. The chaplaincy at St Declan's involved a minimum of teaching one religion class a week and the Legion of Mary required attendance at a weekly meeting.

The most difficult chore I had was looking after the 'Poor Box'. This consisted of the weekly contents of the various shrines in the church. Normally this revenue, which could be considerable, would be used to help pay off the church/parish debt. However there was much unemployment and poverty in the parish and it was used as a kind of safety net to help those whom the St Vincent de Paul Conference could not adequately provide for. Apart from being poor, these unfortunate people were hopeless managers. It was my job in dispensing the Poor Box to ensure that some of these families had adequate food by the end of each week. Cecil had to do likewise and, while he issued food vouchers to nominated shops, I distributed the money.

Invariably we had to cope with some con-men and indeed con-women. One of these really annoyed Cecil and myself. He was comfortable, relative to the overall standard of living in the parish, and resided in a neat, red-brick house in the small section of the parish which did not consist of corporation housing. He treated Cecil and me as simply additional sources of income and invariably his requests were far too inflated for me to accede to. He wrote to the archbishop on a number of occasions complaining that we were not caring for the poor as we should. Eventually a member of the family crashed his car. He applied to Cecil and me for £650 to buy a good second-hand car, as he alleged that if he travelled to work by bus he suffered from headaches. We told him that the resources available to us could not be used in this way.

Not to be outdone, this gentleman requested an interview with the archbishop whom he met in due course and received a cheque for £650. He bought an almost new second-hand car and a few days later drove it around to show it to Cecil and myself. Before leaving he informed us that he had told the archbishop how unhelpful we had been to him. At that time all I could afford to run was a Heinkel Scooter and Cecil had bought his first car only a year earlier.

In effect ours was the only presbytery in the parish. Such was the procession of people to the door and the incessant ringing of the telephone, in order to relax, even when off-duty, Cecil and I had to leave the presbytery. We invariably availed of the hospitality of Jack and Bridie O'Meara who kept a 'safe house' for us further up the road. Both of us became life-long friends of that delightful couple.

Much of the fun among the priests centred on Steve Greene. His high intelligence was not matched by any guile whatsoever. It was very easy to wind him up. He wrongly assumed that he was living under the shadow of his predecessor, Fr 'Flash' Kavanagh, so-called because of the speed at which he celebrated Mass! 'Flash', as he was universally known, had run St Finbar's Hall as a kind of poor relation to the Theatre Royal. He was friendly with Dublin's show-biz folk and socialised with them. Something of a rake, he had a wonderful *rapport* with the poor and his generosity to them was a byword. Parishioners continually expressed their affection for 'Flash' and his memory. While the rest of us considered this to be only right and proper, Steve mistakenly believed it implied in some way that he had not adequately filled 'Flash's' shoes.

Steve was not very adept at extricating himself from awkward or embarrassing situations. The canon generously hosted a number of dinners for us during the year: the confirmation dinner, a dinner at the beginning and end of the annual mission and a few others. When it came to the coffee, he would ask if we would like him to play the violin. To hear him play was indescribable. After listening once we all decided not to be a captive audience ever again. So an hour and a half after each clerical dinner began, urgent calls would start coming in for each of us, except for Steve who time and time again would forget to tip off his housekeeper to send for him urgently. He would then have to sit and listen as the canon ploughed his way through a sheaf of music.

At one stage Steve suspected that communism was getting a grip on the parish and he said to the rest of us that if we did not mind that he would take the pulpit at all Masses during the following three Sundays. We persuaded him to take six. Steve, as usual, did a superb job, although I was not quite sure what the men and women of Cabra West made of the Hegelian dialectic of thesis, antithesis, and synthesis!

From the priests' point of view, St Finbar's Hall was the 'biggest headache' in the parish. It was a hive of activity: with bingo, classes for Irish dancing and 'show-girl' dancing, sessions for bands of all kinds, socials, teenage dances and concerts. Rows between the various groups, using the hall, seemed to go on all the time. There was even the occasional fist-fight in the hall. We managed to keep all of this well away from the ears of the canon, as his reaction would be to close down the hall.

One of the lighter incidents, I recall, in connection with the hall concerned the canon. Steve wisely ensured that he was never encouraged to attend any of the almost nightly functions in the hall. This suited the canon as he rose early and retired early. However, each year Steve put on a gala Christmas show which, apart from a few professional artists, was a show-case for the talent of those using the hall. One of the most popular classes was run by two ladies who had been 'Royalettes' in the old Theatre Royal. They held sessions in 'show-girl dancing' for under 12, under 14 and under 16 girls. These classes were very useful, as apart from the dancing skills, they taught the young girls a great deal about poise and posture.

At the Christmas show in question, we were all in the front row, the canon in the middle and his curates on either side of him. He took a child-like pleasure in appearing in public with his curates around him! The dance routines of the under 12, under 14 and under 16 'show-girls' were interspersed through-out the programme. All the young ladies wore the briefest of briefs and when they twirled on their toes seemed to have little underneath. Before the end of the show we knew that the canon strongly disapproved of their performances and he went home without saying a word. When we arrived in the sacristy on the following morning for our respective Masses, there was a message that he wished us to attend a meeting in the parochial house at noon. We were fairly certain of what was on his mind and, because we were very fond of the old man, agreed not to say anything lest we upset him further.

In due course we arrived at the parochial house and we were ushered into his room. He was sitting at his desk, and did not invite us to sit down. Beginning with the line in Scripture about Christ inviting the little ones to come to him … he embarked on a tirade accusing us of leading all the little ones astray in pro-moting the development of their sexual instincts before their time. To make it worse, he was in tears. I thought Steve, who put so much time and effort into running the hall, would burst with indignation but he managed to restrain himself. However, Cecil could not remain staring into the middle distance like the rest of us and began, as he frequently did, to grin. The old man then lost his temper and ordered us to leave his house as we were a disgrace to the parish, the diocese and the country!

During my two and a half years in Cabra West, I assisted at
about a hundred marriages. Nearly all of them were marriages
of teenagers and quite a few were ARPs. This was the sign we
put after marriages where the young lady was already pregnant.
I am sure that, like all marriages, they had their rocky passages
but I am not aware that any have been annulled subsequently.
The level of maturity of those teenage working girls was remarkable. Certainly it was such that I seldom met subsequently
even in women graduates in their mid to late twenties from
middle-class families. It seems a little hardship has its advantages
as well as its disadvantages.

Although time consuming, I attended the reception of every
marriage I conducted. This is a practice I have always followed. I
discovered that there is a deep appreciation of a priest's presence
on such occasions. In Cabra West, these receptions varied a lot.
On one occasion after marrying a couple, I had to give the
bridegroom a loan to pay for the reception. I attended many
receptions in small corporation houses in Cabra West, Finglas
West and Crumlin.

One of the most popular venues for Cabra West couples was
the 'Glenbeigh' off the Old Cabra Road. The proprietor had divided
a large, ground-floor room with a partition and had placed a
piano on each side. The menu was always the same: celery soup,
chicken and ham, trifle, a slice of wedding cake and a cup of tea.
About forty people would be seated at forms at two long tables.
Sometimes it was a job to get the men in from the bar and even
when the meal had started, some of them would be getting up
from the table and going to the bar to have their drinks replen-
ished. Smart remarks were tossed around incessantly. I remember
one man saying to me as I spoke to his companion: 'Never mind
that fellow Father. He'd ate the lamb of God.' On another occasion the soup was slow in coming and a man up the table from
me began to eat a piece of celery with a small green leaf on top of
it. One gentleman opposite me said to his friend: 'Christ! The
fellow up there is so hungry he is eating the flowers.'

Frequently two receptions would be held at the same time on

either side of the partition. On a few occasions, my life-long friend, Fr Mick Cleary, then a reader in Clogher Road parish, was present at a reception on one side while I was on the other. On one such occasion, Michael, who even then was a popular and well-known figure, was called upon to sing. He never required much prompting and sang his party piece 'The Old Bog Road'. My group listened with appreciation. They then called on me for a song. I was not going to let Cleary get away with all the kudos of the situation and rendered my party piece 'The Rose of Tralee'. Word got around about this and thereafter 'The Rose of Tralee' was *de rigueur* at all wedding receptions I attended.

At every wedding reception, with or without Mass, I availed of the opportunity to get across a worthwhile message. I based my comments on a splendid summary of the meaning of Christian marriage contained in the *Marriage Ritual* then in use. As the young couples were always very nervous, I was always aware that it was really those attending the ceremony I was addressing. I quickly learned that at the wedding reception one had to be brief, thank everybody in sight, make a few flippant remarks and above all end and sit down as the company was laughing at the last joke. Marriages were attended by persons of all ages and of greatly differing attitudes so that the more bland a joke was and in keeping with the ethos of the time, the more suitable it would be. I used as my punch-line a joke given to me by Cecil on my way out to conduct my first marriage in Cabra West

Owing to a number of sudden and unexpected deaths among parish priests in the winter of 1962, a supplementary 'Honours List' was issued in the first week of December. I found myself on it again and I was to succeed my friend, Fr Maurice O'Moore, who also some years earlier had cut his teeth in Cabra West, as curate in Aughrim-Greenane. I was embarrassed by the reaction of the people to this news. They were fiercely loyal to their priests and the poorer they were the greater their loyalty and affection. I had had responsibility for the most deprived section of the parish and with the assistance of the residents and boys and girls of the Legion of Mary had worked to make a two-storey house given to us by the Corporation a kind of community centre for that area. Mainly to stop the house being systematically vandalised, we erected a beautiful Marian shrine at the gable of the house. These fellow-workers were very upset at my transfer and some to my consternation even cried. The going-away presents they gave me were, relative to their resources, exceedingly generous. I was glad the change had to be completed within a week. With a heavy heart I headed for Greenane. I knew I would miss for some time to come the warm-hearted people of Cabra West and my ever-supportive colleagues. I was in no doubt that I had received a splendid in-training education on life and ministry in one of the larger, city, working-class parishes.

CHAPTER 5

Most Sacred Heart, Aughrim-Greenane
1962-1964

In the first week of December 1962 I was transferred from the parish of Cabra West in Dublin to Aughrim-Greenane in County Wicklow. The difference between the two parishes could scarcely have been greater. Cabra West was near the city centre; Aughrim-Greenane in South Wicklow bordered on the diocese of Ferns on one side and Kildare and Leighlin on the other. One was a bustling, working-class parish of some 16,000 people, the other, spread for more than 20 miles over the undulating foothills of Lugnaquilla, Ballinacor and Kirikee mountains, had less than 750 residents.

I was fortunate to have completed the transfer within the second week of December as heavy snowfalls subsequently made transport in and out of Greenane in Glenmalure at my end of the parish impossible. The winter of 1962-3 had arrived, generally regarded with that of 1946-47 as one of the worst in living memory. Having driven my Morris Minor into Glenmalure in mid-December I was not able to drive it out again until the first week in March. There were persistent heavy snowfalls, almost continuous frost and the only access to Glenmalure was over two very steep hills. Movement for everyone in the area was at times well-nigh impossible. The attendance at my two Masses on Christmas Day must have been the smallest anywhere in Ireland. The collections at the two Masses realised £1 10s 8½d (about two Euro!).

The inclement weather made physical conditions difficult. The water supply to the house broke down. Twice each day I had to traverse two fields under two feet of snow to get a bucket of water from a mountain stream. Wood had to be chopped to keep a fire going. For two weeks I had no electricity and depended on candles for light.

On the positive side Mrs Nora Byrne, the wife of a local forester, who resided a mile and a half away walked in on most days and prepared a hot meal in the middle of the day. For about two months this consisted solely of potatoes and bully beef from tins, an ample supply of which I was able to get from the only store within four miles. This was owned by a family, named Brownriggs. They were Plymouth Brethren who all the year round lived the kind of reclusive existence I was then enduring. A local farmer provided me with a bottle of milk each morning. The hill-farmers lost nearly all their sheep. Among the people scattered around the countryside there was a strong sense of community in the face of the challenges posed by the cruel weather conditions. The people were particularly helpful and supportive of me all the time and referred to me as 'our priest'.

I was able to keep in touch with the outside world through radio. Each eight or nine days I would receive a bundle of mail and a week's supply of the daily newspaper, which I would read in sequence. One way, I recall, in which I whiled away my time was by reading Catholic Truth Society pamphlets. Fr Des Howett, a former curate, had a hobby of collecting these in the way other people collect stamps and there were hundreds of them on every conceivable topic in the house.

Notwithstanding such a 'baptism of fire', my most vivid memory of Aughrim-Greenane was my association with Fr George Henry. George, as he was known in the archdiocese, was parish priest in Aughrim-Greenane for a year before I was appointed his curate. On being informed of my appointment he sought me out before I had time to present myself to him. I shall never forget our first meeting. I was immediately reminded of Charlie Chaplin. He was the same size as the legendary comedian. His actions: hand and head movements were quite jerky, and he walked very rapidly. He was bald as an egg, had rimless glasses half-way down his nose, was never without a pleasant grin and spoke in a very loud voice.

George told me he had been informed that I was 'an expert in Aristotelian philosophy' and suggested that I accompany him down to Aughrim a few days later so that he could introduce me to a few of the parishioners. In due course we arrived in the village and on entering each of the three public-houses we shook hands with a number of forestry workers having a drink on their way home after work. They were somewhat bemused when George, after introducing me, confided to each of them that the new curate was 'an expert in Aristotelian philosophy'.

On the first Sunday in Greenane George told me he would come over, preach at the 11 o'clock Mass and introduce me to the congregation. Although he was a native of Blackrock, he was the quintessential 'Dub'. He had a sharp wit, was ever full of fun and with a fund of smart remarks. For him anybody outside Dublin was a 'Culchie'. And as he confided to me on more than one occasion the 'Cork and Kerry Culchies were the worst of the lot'.

In his sermon George telescoped Scriptural quotations in a manner I never heard before or since. He suggested, as the collections should be better, thereafter silver would be expected at all collections (at that time a 3d piece was silver). He then introduced me whom he described as a Kerry 'Culchie', stressing that he was a 'Dub' for whom finding himself in Rathfarnham was like being in the 'Sticks'. He told them that he would not know the difference between a bull and a cow but with a theatrical gesture towards me he said: 'But that fellow there would.' George had a cup of tea after Mass and decamped to Aughrim. The next time I laid an eye on him was in the *Irish Independent*, where in an issue at the end of January there was a picture of George as he was being taken on a tractor to visit a seriously ill farmer through snow-covered fields.

After the snow disappeared from Glenmalure about mid-March I came to know and like George very much. Whenever he entered a room or joined a group of people the level of gaiety and joy lifted appreciably. However, when he was around there never was a dull moment. He had a number of hobbies. An avid soccer follower, he was a dedicated supporter of Shamrock Rovers and conversely had contempt for the GAA and the Irish language, both of which he regarded as 'Culchie' pursuits. But his abiding passion was Music Hall entertainment. He became a magician and was accepted into the magicians' circle. In addition he was a competent ventriloquist and he had a good singing voice. He dressed up appropriately when performing in these various roles. When he was in a 'showing-off' mood and that was most of the time he brought his case of props with him. These he had along when after the snow melted and normality returned to the hills around Greenane he brought me to the three one-roomed, one-teacher schools, of which I was to be the manager. In the first of these a beautiful red-head in her mid-twenties faced 26 boys and girls, belonging to all classes from Babies to 6th class. After introducing me to the teacher, George donned his theatrical garb and a Tommy Cooper fez hat. He went straight into his magician's act. To the intense embarrassment of the teacher, and indeed everybody else, this included discovering pennies under her skirt! He ended his ventriloquist stint by showing the teacher, again to her embarrassment, the silk underwear of his ventriloquist doll. It was all Music Hall burlesque and George loved it.

Apart from carrying out his essential duties George did not spend much time around Aughrim. The call of the city was too much. On most weekdays having celebrated his 8 o'clock Mass in the parish church and attended to whatever parish business was to hand he headed for Dublin. Sometimes he would be in such a hurry to leave for Dublin that he would begin Mass five or even ten minutes before 8. Information about this was unfailingly reported to archbishop's house. Each evening having had his tea with his two sisters in their old home he returned to Aughrim at about 8 o'clock. Much of his time in Dublin, apart from an occasional Shamrock Rovers match, was spent in organising and putting on shows for one charity or another. He had gathered around him a troupe of performers. These were mostly young women who were past pupils of the school conducted by the Holy Faith Sisters in Glasnevin where he had been school-chaplain for many years.

My predecessor had diplomatically succeeded in keeping George out of his end of the parish. However, George persuaded me to let him put on one of his shows to raise funds for Kirikee National School in Glenmalure. The school hall was packed and everybody had a most enjoyable night. The only problem was that putting George on stage was one thing, getting him off it was something else. We had to end the show by pretending that the curtain had accidentally fallen down. He was delighted with the night and was indefatigable that we should have another which we had. This time, as well as acting as MC, he did his magician's act, his ventriloquist act and sang a few duets with Fr Jerry O'Brien (present parish priest of Aughrim!). Only a few of his troupe ventured down to Glenmalure with him on this second occasion. It was almost a one-man show. He crowned his performance with the well-known monologue about the G.I. being reminded of his religion by a pack of cards. When George came to the five of clubs he said: 'the five of clubs: the five virgins'. And looking down at the audience added: 'Ha, ha, I'm sure there are very few virgins here!'

During my time in Aughrim-Greenane I helped George conduct a voluminous correspondence with Archbishop John Charles McQuaid. At that time it was the practice of the arch-bishop when he received a signed letter of complaint to refer the letter to the relevant parish priest. George was scarcely a month in the parish before one or two such letters were winging their way to archbishop's house each week. The complaints about George ranged from the sublime to the ridiculous – mostly the ridiculous. They were immediately returned to George as follows:

> Dear Fr Henry,
> Please comment on the enclosed.
> Yours etc.
> +John C. McQuaid

George during all his working hours was generally in high good humour. But after receiving one of these 'McQuaid rockets',

as he called them, he would be subdued for some time. After I
joined him in Aughrim-Greenane he quickly adopted a procedure in dealing with them. On returning from Dublin he would
pick up his mail and if one of these 'rockets' was in it he would
ring me to come over to Aughrim at once. When I asked him
why he would simply say: 'An emergency!' By the time I arrived in
Aughrim a half an hour later he would be already in his pyjamas
and in bed. When he opened the front door he was like an
illustration in a Charles Dickens novel, as he wore a strange
head-dress when in bed. He would usher me into his bedroom
where there was a card-table and chair at the end of his bed. We
would spend some time agreeing on what devious spin to put
on our reply to the 'offending letter'. George would give me half
a shilling-bar of chocolate which he always brought from
Dublin. He would then get into bed, enjoy the other half of the
chocolate bar and proceed to read the *Evening Herald*. When I
had finished drafting the reply he would read it and then copy it
out in his own very characteristic, large hand-writing. I would
then have to deliver it to Rathdrum whence there was the quick-
est post back to Dublin.

The contrast between George and his opposite number in the
adjoining parish of Annacurra could not have been more striking. Fr Walter Kane had been a brilliant student in St Patrick's
College, Maynooth, and like most such persons was shy, modest
and rather diffident. He was quietly spoken and devoid of con-
versational patter. For many years he had been teaching theology
in St Peter's College in Wexford. After a heart attack and continuing ill-health he had been appointed to the quiet parish of
Annacurra. He was proficient in a number of European languages, including German, and spent much of his time translating
the works of modern German theologians into English for
American publishers. George could never get much conversation out of Walter who treated him with a tolerant disdain.
Occasionally the county branch of the IFA, Macra na Feirme or
some other national organisation would hold their annual dinner
at Phelan's Hotel in Aughrim. The hotel, though in the village,

was on the south east side of the bridge over the Aughrim river and so in Annacurra parish. All the local clergy, Catholic and Church of Ireland, would be invited to the dinner. At these gatherings, while George would be bustling around trying to impress everybody, Walter Kane would be doing his best to fade into the background. There was a gentleman's agreement whereby the Catholics said the 'Grace before Meals' one year and the Church of Ireland incumbent the next and so on. That year, at the annual dinner which I recall, it was the RCs' turn. When the person presiding called on the parish priest to invoke the blessing George shot up. He was half-way through it when I realised that it was Walter Kane, in whose parish the hotel was situated, who should have said the 'Grace'. When I drew George's attention to this faux pas he shrugged it off as being 'very funny'. Later in the evening George attempted unsuccessfully to engage Walter Kane in conversation. This prompted him to say to me in a very loud stage whisper heard by Walter: 'That Walter Kane. He's odd.'

I served with George for about a year until he was appointed parish priest of Crumlin-Walkinstown. The circumstances surrounding his transfer were extraordinary. It seems that the sisters in the Poor Clare convent at Simmonscourt Road in Donnybrook parish needed financial support for some project. They informed the relevant vicar general, Mgr Charles Hurley, of this. He was aware of George's fund-raising gigs and asked him to help which he did, raising £150. This information was conveyed to the archbishop. At that time the parish of Crumlin was in the throes of establishing what became the parish of Walkinstown. The development costs of the new parish even for this area of 65,000 people were enormous and at that time had to be borne by the mother parish. In casting around for a new parish priest for Crumlin, which had become vacant, the archbishop had fund-raising on his mind and chose George.

George rushed around to tell his many friends and acquaintances and anybody else who cared to listen of his unexpected promotion. I was among the first to learn about it. He rang me and said: 'Instead of you, now I'll have eight curates.' The news of the appointment gave a field day to the cynics among the senior clergy. Some of the quips exchanged reached the ears even of the VGs, if not the archbishop. When Mgr Hurley arrived down in Aughrim to induct Fr Paul Phelan as George's successor, George and I were present. Hurley parked his car opposite the church and as he approached all of us waiting to greet him called out: 'Hey George. The old fellows up in Dublin are saying that Crumlin is the biggest thing yet you pulled out of a hat.'

Another memory of Aughrim-Greenane was the change in the pace of living. Being a curate in Cabra West was all-action; in Aughrim-Greenane it was mostly non-action. However Parkinson's law soon took over. In Cabra West I would prepare and celebrate a funeral Mass, accompany the remains to Glasnevin cemetery, conduct the prayers at the graveside and be back in the presbytery in less than two hours. In Aughrim-Greenane funerals took two full days!

I also experienced loneliness because of the lack of company. In Cabra West I shared a small house with another curate and the housekeeper. The window in my bedroom (the box-room) was just ten yards from a bus-stop where double-deckers screeched to a halt from 7 am to 11 pm. There was almost always somebody at the door or someone being interviewed. In Greenane I met nobody except a few altar-boys who served my daily Mass and Mrs Byrne who came in for seven hours each day. I met parishioners only before or after the two Masses on Sundays. This ensured that I enjoyed all the more the occasional Thursday evenings when I availed of the hospitality of Fr Dick McCullen, CM, and his Vincentian confreres at their theologate at Glenart, near Avoca.

My predecessor had invited five pillars of the half-parish to form a parish council. These were the men who helped with the collection of the Christmas and other offerings or 'Dues', organised fund-raising, the annual sports day, a community water scheme then in progress and any other project undertaken locally. On the first Sunday of each month I would announce a meeting of the parish council for 9 o'clock on the following night. At the first three meetings I noticed they all arrived just ten minutes after closing-time in Byrne's pub in Greenane. When I suggested that I would announce the meeting for 10.30 in future there was horror all round. All of them, it seems, had assured their wives that on the first Monday from 9 onwards they were up in the presbytery with the young priest who was a 'Pioneer'.

These meetings were most enjoyable. Before she left on the Monday afternoon Mrs Byrne would prepare a plentiful supply of ham sandwiches. When the 'councillors' arrived I would make the tea. Thereafter we played cards until the small hours. During these sessions I absorbed a great deal of sound advice and practical wisdom, of which I was in dire need.

As elsewhere the main source of the priest's income was the 'Dues': at Christmas and Easter. In Greenane there were two other collections: the Oats collection in the spring and the Hay collection in the autumn. These referred back to the time when the curate's transport consisted of a pony and trap. Having arrived in Greenane with the reformist zeal characteristic of youth I told the parish council that I regarded the practice of reading out the names of those who contributed to the various collections together with the amount of their offerings as outdated and indeed barbaric! They insisted that to abolish the practice would be disastrous and would reduce my income, one of the lowest in the archdiocese, by about 50%. I was persuaded to let the arrangement continue until I had seen how it worked out in practice. Reluctantly I had to admit that in this instance their advice, as always, was soundly based. Notwithstanding their advice, there was one reform which I was determined to carry out. When I read the Dues list, prepared by the council, I noted that the handful of large farmers, professional people and shop-keepers from the Rathdrum district who attended our Sunday Masses and a retired Trinity College Dublin professor were given their full Christian names. At the same time widows, forestry workers, farm labourers and county council workers, who were just as generous relatively speaking with their 'widow's mites' of 10/- and 5/-, were not given that courtesy.

Coming from a strong egalitarian background I put this right. Whenever subsequently I read out the 'Dues list' this caused considerable merriment which I pretended not to notice lest it got out of hand.

Looking back I now realise that the friendship of these members of the parish council was a truly remarkable experience. I shall never forget their courtesy, kindness and help.

Life with Fr Paul Phelan, George's successor, was different. Paul scarcely ever left Aughrim. He socialised a great deal with his neighbours. His favourite pastime was playing cards and he was a member of every card-school in the village. He publicly expressed his intention to spend the rest of his life in Aughrim which he did except for the final few months. Despite being a chain-smoker he lived to a great age.

When Paul arrived in Aughrim he brought a housekeeper with him. At the best of times he was not very talkative to her nor indeed anybody else. She also sorely missed her friends in Dublin and after two months of virtual isolation decamped. Paul boasted he could cope without any domestic help. He did so but progressively his personal appearance and the state of the parochial house bore evidence to his bachelor lifestyle.

The maintenance of the parish plant in my half of the parish – the church, three single-teacher schools, parish hall and pres-bytery – was one of my major responsibilities. My predecessor, Fr Maurice O'Moore, had been particularly attentive in this regard. I continued the good work. I replaced a septic tank near the presbytery and I had the Floods of Clonroche in County Wexford bore a 40 foot well to ensure a supply of clear water to the presbytery. I kept one of the Floods for two weeks until the job was completed. I also supervised the completion of a group water-scheme in Glenmalure which had been initiated by Maurice O'Moore.

I effected a number of minor improvements in the church and church grounds. However, the main problem here was the roof. It was sagging noticeably in a few places and leaked in inclement weather. This was not surprising. The local people, who had long memories, were able to tell me that the church had been built in 1801. It was built by a native of Gorey, Fr John Kavanagh, a former chaplain in the French navy and then a curate in Rathdrum. Fr Kavanagh built it to replace a chapel which stood not far away 'on the brow of Ballinacor'. This had been burnt in 1798 by the Protestant yeomen of Rathdrum. Fr Kavanagh, who eventually died as parish priest of Rathdrum in 1825, was buried at the south side of Greenane church where a tomb slab with Latin inscription marks the grave and links those stormy times with the present.

Our parish spring and autumn draws were well supported by neighbouring parishes. However I was somewhat anxious about raising the considerable sum required for repairing the roof. I worried out loud about it at a dinner with my classmates and Fr Colm Gallagher told me that his brother, Vincent, a well-known architect, would provide me with free advice on the matter. In due course Vincent telephoned. He said he would be down on the coming Friday, have lunch and do a survey. I invited him to meet me at a hotel in Avoca but he insisted he wished to have the same lunch as I was having in the presbytery. His lunch on that Friday of two fried eggs, potatoes, salt and a glass of milk was in sharp contrast to the Jaguar in which he arrived! True to his word Vincent provided me with a comprehensive report on the church in general and the roof in particular. Because of my early departure from the parish that was as far as I got to replacing the roof!

As soon as the snow had disappeared from the Glen in 1963 I called on the Reverend James A. Farrar, the local Church of Ireland incumbent who resided with a young family at Ballinatone on the road to Ballinaclash. He had a well-kept manse but the number of the families in his parish did not exceed single figures. I invited him to tea in my presbytery. He accepted the invitation and reciprocated the gesture. His most important annual social event was a Garden Fete which he organised on the 15th of August on the extensive lawns of the manse. Some of the stalls were provided and run by my parish-

ioners, nearly all of whom attended. I spent most of the day at
the Fete and met half the Protestants of Counties Wexford and
Wicklow who turned up in admirable numbers to support him.

On a Sunday in June each summer the people of Greenane
organised a parish sports. Captain William Kemmis, the resident Protestant landlord, gave the use of his Glebe field for the
occasion. However, each year the curate had personally to request the use of the field. Sports day at Greenane was regarded
as a red-letter day throughout the district. It was a joyful and
wonderful occasion with marquees, meals, stalls, school sports
day, a couple of marching bands and a football match.

The annual football match was initiated by Fr Charlie Troy
and the cup he presented, called 'The Priest's Cup', was played
for each year. Charlie held the record for spending the longest
curacy in Greenane: over eight years. Until the advent of John C.
McQuaid to the see of Dublin Greenane was treated as the
'Siberia' of the archdiocese. Almost without exception the
priests who served as curates there were strong and all too often
irresponsible supporters of the anti-treatyites before, during and
after the civil war, including Fr Bill Lillis who had served as a
judge in the Sinn Féin courts in 1920-21. To their credit the Irish
bishops urged unambiguous acceptance of the democratically
expressed support by the people for the Anglo-Irish treaty, even
though tens of thousands of decent and principled men and
women regarded that as an affront. In the confused period between the vote in Dáil Éireann approving the treaty in January
1922 and the outbreak of civil war in the following June Charlie,
then a newly-ordained priest, was one of the speakers in his
native Listowel at a giant rally opposing the treaty. This serious
indiscretion was reported to Archbishop Edward Byrne by the
parish priest of Ballybunion. I discovered this while researching
in the State Paper Office in 1970. Soon afterwards I met Charlie
on our annual diocesan retreat and disabused him of his life-
long conviction that it was William T. Cosgrave who had reported
him. When John C. McQuaid became archbishop all these
priests were given a fresh start.

After Paul's induction I anticipated being three more years in Greenane. To ensure that I had something to occupy myself with during the coming winters I wrote to the archbishop requesting permission to enroll at UCD to take an MA in philosophy over a two-year period. By return of post he commended my initiative and suggested I discuss the matter with Mgr John D. Horgan, dean of the faculty of philosophy.

From the time I had spent earlier at UCD I was aware that John Horgan had an immense interest in his students and was most approachable. He had a photographic memory and prided himself on his ability to know every one of the hundreds of students who passed through his classes by their Christian names. In due course I met him. He suggested I prepare a thesis in his own subject of metaphysics on 'The concept of being'. Besides giving me an extensive reading list, he told me to ensure that I could read relevant articles and studies in French and German.

'The Horg', as we affectionately knew him, gave me some of the books he wanted me to read. I also had a few sessions with him towards the end of the year. These, however, were not very useful, as all he seemed eager to do was have a good gossip about the diocese. Then before Christmas he told me he had had a discussion with the archbishop and they had decided I should join him in the department of metaphysics as a tutor. I was to continue with the MA thesis and if that went well to pursue further studies in Louvain. Soon afterwards he had me appointed a tutor in metaphysics for a two-year period at £450 per annum. And he told me that when the next list of diocesan changes came out I would be transferred to some appointment nearer to UCD.

CHAPTER 6

St Mary's Convent, Donnybrook
1964-1965

In February 1964 I was appointed chaplain to St Mary's Convent, Donnybrook. St Mary's was established in 1833 by the Sisters of Charity, generally known as the Irish Sisters of Charity. Today with significant State assistance the Sisters provide a residential centre for women, a social service centre, a day centre for the elderly, visitation of the sick and poor and a residential centre for the female elderly. For the first 150 years of the convent's history, the Sisters provided a refuge for homeless and penniless women, a substantial minority of whom were, as they always referred to them, 'Magdalens'. Hence the convent was known as 'The Magdalen Home in Donnybrook'.

Until some years ago the Sisters financed their institution mainly with the help of generous donations, legacies, an annual appeal for the Home and income realised from the laundry run by both the Sisters and the women sheltering in the Home. In 1964 there were about a hundred women in the Home, most of whom were in their sixties, seventies and eighties and many of them had spent most of their lives in St Mary's. About twenty younger women came and went every two or three months. On entering, they would generally be in a wretched condition but with care and medical attention would be transformed after a few months when once again they would decamp for some time. I was told by the Sisters, and noted this myself, that, as in the case of the archetypal Mary Magdalen, the more wayward the women were in their youth the more pious and religious they tended to become as they grew older.

My duties at St Mary's were to celebrate Mass at 7 am Monday to Friday, at 7.45 on Saturday and Sunday and hear

Confessions for an hour and a half every Saturday evening. I also helped out on special occasions such as feast days, the Forty Hours Adoration of the Blessed Sacrament, the *Corpus Christi* procession, etc. For this I received £200 per annum and my breakfast each morning.

Apart from religious services I met the women only on festive occasions or at Easter and Christmas. At Christmas the Sisters had a professional actor or producer help the women put on a show. Local dignitaries and especially those who supported St Mary's throughout the year would be honoured guests. The women, both those on the stage and in front of it, would be at their most glamorous. On one occasion I congratulated one of the young women a Marilyn Munroe lookalike as quite a few of them were on her appearance. She replied good naturedly: 'Father, I would not do any business, if I had not my war paint on!'

While at St Mary's I became acutely aware of genuine and practical compassion for the women who sheltered in it. This was especially true of the Sisters but it was also true of the Gardaí and members of the judiciary. I was privy to a number of situations where this was evident.

One incident I recall concerned a young woman who was convicted of infanticide. The circumstances of the case were particularly sad. At that time the Sisters and the Gardaí did everything they could to ensure that women were not sent to prison. In this instance at the request of the Sisters, I attended the proceedings in Green Street Criminal Court and brought a message to the judge from the Sisters that the young woman who had taken refuge with them had her best chance of being rehabilitated in St Mary's rather than in prison and that they guaranteed that if given into their care she would remain with them until her sentence had been completed. In this instance as well as every other one I was aware of the detectives who investigated the case and the court officials were most helpful, as without exception they, as well as the Sisters, were very reluctant to see women in prison.

After presenting myself to the mother superior of St Mary's I called on Fr C. P. (Paddy) Crean, the parish priest in Donnybrook, and offered to help in any way that was required. In the event, apart from the Forty Hours devotion, the *Corpus Christi* procession and a few other occasions, I was not called to do so, as the parish was well-staffed. Crean was an imposing figure, over six feet tall, straight as a ramrod and somewhat pompous. He served as a chaplain with the British army in World War II and later in the Irish army, eventually becoming the head chaplain before being appointed to Donnybrook.

As a member, albeit the most junior one, of the parish team I was invited to the various dinners hosted by the parish priest throughout the year. Paddy Crean was an excellent host and these were very enjoyable occasions. The dinners for the missioners at the beginning and end of the annual mission were particularly so. At one of these I incurred Crean's displeasure. It was the first Sunday in September and I requested permission to leave early to get to the All-Ireland hurling final in Croke Park. As if this was not enough, during the meal he asked me if I knew Fr Tom Stack. I told him that Tom was a close friend, a brilliant conversationalist, with an addiction to seeking out and engaging interesting persons and had never been known to underestimate himself. He then told the company that while visiting a number of parishioners during the week who were distinguished members of the Irish legal profession – judges and senior barristers – nearly all of them had been recently visited socially by this Fr Stack! And in one residence a judge's wife had said to him: 'Fr Crean. You will have to join us some evening when we are having Fr Stack for dinner' I told Crean I thought that was very funny, to which he replied: 'Father, I do not find it a bit amusing.' I was left in no doubt about that fact when, as I left for Croke Park, he said: 'Give our best regards to all the bog-trotters.'

One of my first chores after reporting to St Mary's was to obtain accommodation. Fr Steve Clancy, one of the curates in Donnybrook, gave me a list of a few suitable places, but they were fully occupied. Then, at the request of the mother superior,

a Garda superintendent's widow provided me with accommod-
ation. She already had a priest paying-guest, Fr Tom Kelly, SM.
He was English and his order had sent him to UCD to obtain a
BA in languages with a view to teaching in one of their schools.
Tom was in his third and final year, a good student and very
pleasant company.

About three months later I had a telephone call from Fr
Dermot O'Neill. He was a curate in Foxrock and had been told
by a mutual friend, Fr Noel Madden, about my situation. He
invited me to occupy two spare rooms which he had and I
moved at once to Foxrock.

I regard this move as one of the many fortunate things that
have happened to me throughout my life. Dermot was one of
the happiest persons I ever met. From the time he got out of bed
in the morning until he retired he had a pleasant smile. A person
of remarkable intelligence, he had numerous hobbies: hill-walk-
ing, cycling, bee-keeping, gardening, accordion-playing and
carpentry. He always counselled taking 'the long view' and I
learned a great deal from him during my year residing in
Foxrock. One of his most impressive qualities was his concern
for the 'underdog'. For over ten years he was in charge of a
youth club which catered for one of the most deprived areas of
the city. Quite a few of its members were youngsters who 'lived
rough' and survived on a share of the earnings of prostitutes for
whom they pimped. As adults they drifted into criminality.
However, Dermot's boys never forgot him. When out of jail they
paid him a weekly visit for help.

I supplied for Dermot when he was on holiday but I was not
asked to do much more in the parish, as it was well staffed.
Dermot's two colleagues were as different as chalk and cheese,
the one tended to be a confirmed optimist, the other a confirmed
pessimist, and he regaled me with stories of amusing situations
which this led to. The anecdote which I recall as summing up the
relationship between the priests in the parish relates to a visit
Dermot made to the parish priest, Fr Anthony Camac. He had
visited Camac who was confined to bed with a heart condition.

Camac was a great favourite with the priests and people, had an infectious sense of humour and loved company. When he was ill the curates enjoyed dropping in for a chat. On the occasion in question Dermot discovered that his two colleagues had been in to see Camac earlier in the day. The old man looked very tired. He pointed to two rows of tablets next to the bed, one consisted of green tablets, the other of red. With a twinkle in his eye he said: 'Fr O'Neill, the green tablets are known as "downers", the red ones as "uppers". After Fr O'Connell has been in with me I have to take two of the green tablets to calm me down and after Fr Mahon has been in I have to take two of the red ones to buck me up'.

In the meantime I had not made much progress with the MA thesis. Soon after I had transferred to Dublin Mgr Horgan told me that he had requested Fr Des Connell to take over supervision of my thesis. At that time the staff of the department of metaphysics in UCD was: Professor: Mgr John D. Horgan, Lecturer: Fr Desmond Connell, Assistant lecturer: Dr Patrick Masterson and Tutor: Fr J. Anthony Gaughan. I soon discovered that Des did not relish his new responsibility. It was difficult to meet him and when I did succeed it was not in Earlsfort Terrace but in his residence in Glasnevin after his evening meal. I continued to read widely on the subject and drafted some notes but I had not identified any specific aspect of the very wide subject or focused on an angle I could concentrate on.

After some months owing to my own ineptitude and a lack of direction or assistance from Des, I became quite frustrated. After showing him a chapter I had written he handed it back to me with the comment: 'It would not even pass 1st Arts.' This led to a heated exchange.

A week later Paddy Masterson met me in Earlsfort Terrace in an agitated state. He told me he had come from a meeting with the 'Mons' and Des. Apparently they had decided to write to the archbishop to have me re-assigned to parish work immediately.

Paddy objected that it would be unfair not to allow me to complete the MA and he undertook to take over its supervision.

He was true to his word and during the following four months I was able with his generous assistance to complete 'The metaphysical value and importance of the concept of being'. In due course I was conferred with the degree. Subsequently I published the thesis and it was reviewed favourably.

I was exceedingly grateful to Paddy and invited him and his charming wife, Frankie, during the early years of their marriage to have the occasional meal at my presbytery in East Wall. Subsequently I watched with great interest and pleasure his remarkable career as a professor and dean of the philosophy faculty in UCD, later his tenure of the presidency of UCD and eventually becoming principal of the European University Institute in Florence. The splendid work he did in developing UCD should be better known. But then Paddy is as unassuming as he is brilliant and likeable.

CHAPTER 7

St Joseph's, East Wall
1965-1967

In June 1965 I was appointed a curate in St Joseph's, East Wall. The parish extended from the North Strand down to and including the docks area. It had been cut off from the parish of St Laurence O'Toole, Seville Place, and constituted as a separate parish in 1941. Services were conducted in a temporary church in Church Road from 1919 until 1956 when the present parish church of St Joseph's was completed.

When I arrived in the parish, the first stage of the new style planned-giving campaign, involving the pledging of contributions, had been launched and there remained the task of organising the collection of the contributions pledged. A collector had to be assigned to each twenty homes in the parish who delivered weekly or monthly contributions to a supervisor. The supervisor then brought these to a weekly meeting where they were registered with a view to acknowledging them every quarter. It was not difficult to set up and supervise this 'Outdoor Collection', as it was called, as the people derived a great deal of satisfaction at having at long last their beautiful new parish church.

Like my fellow curates: Fr Jim Fingleton and Fr Eugene McCarney (later Fr Gerry Canning), I had responsibility for a daily Mass – mine was 8 am – the usual confessions, Masses and preaching every weekend and a district which included six hundred families.

The curates in East Wall were kept very busy. Every week each curate on his two duty days provided a twenty-four service. The parishioners availed of this and called on the priest for every conceivable service. The elderly, the infirm, and the sick were cared for in their homes and there was a high proportion of them right across the parish. I had twenty-eight persons on my list of the house-bound for confession and communion once a month.

January, February and early March were very difficult months for the elderly. Besides the severe weather, air pollution often reached a high level. Throughout the year, Roadstone Ireland, Collen Brothers and a number of other heavy and dirty industries in the area polluted the atmosphere. But when thick fog enveloped the district, as it occasionally did in the winter and early spring, the pollution was quite obnoxious and seriously affected parishioners who had asthma and chest infections. In fact, this pollution was probably the main reason for the high incidence of chest and lung illnesses in the area.

Apart from my specifically priestly duties, I had a number of extra tasks which I inherited from my predecessor, Fr Cronan Byrne. These were mainly chaplaincies – to the girls' national school, the parish troop of the Catholic Girl Guides, the St Vincent de Paul Society, and the Women's Sodality. I also had responsibility for the parish hall and a food centre.

The staff of the girls' school consisted of two Irish Sisters of Charity and six lay teachers. The senior nun was both principal and manager. It was a very well run school. I taught religion to a different class each week and afterwards spent some time in the staff room. My chaplaincy to the girl guides involved only a brief visit to the weekly meeting to encourage the excellent leaders. The girl guides were drawn from the lower middle class end of the parish and were a very well-behaved group.

The weekly meeting I enjoyed attending most was that of the St Vincent de Paul conference. There was plenty for the members to do, as there was a great deal of poverty in the parish. The members were nearly all civil servants from the Clontarf area and had been active in the society since leaving their secondary school, St Joseph's CBS, Marino. Their generosity with their time and genuine sympathy for those they helped was edifying. Tim Cahill, a native of Glenbeigh and then chairman of the Labour Court, was the grand old man of the conference. Meticulously

dressed and always with a bow tie, by his never-failing attendance at meetings he gave wonderful example to the junior
members.

I also inherited responsibility for the parish hall from my
predecessor. Functions of all kinds were held in it and not a few
for charitable causes. East Wall was a very close-knit community.
Nearly everybody seemed to be related to everybody else. The
sense of community was such that, although a mere fifteen minute
walk from the city centre, it could have been a small village in the
heart of the country. Thus whenever tragedy, hardship or serious illness struck a family, neighbours rallied around and held a
collection or a function to relieve their distress.

There were the usual difficulties and protests one met in
trying to please everybody in running the hall. There was one
protest, however, which I considered somewhat bizarre. A number of my priest friends were running Bingo in their parishes to
raise funds. I saw how successful and popular these were. The
clientele, mainly women, who attended them seemed to enjoy
them very much. I put on Bingo in the hall every Wednesday
and Sunday night. We ran it on non-profit lines, giving back in
prizes all the money we took at the door save what was necessary to cover our expenses – cost of Bingo cards, tea, biscuits, etc.
The Bingo nights were immensely popular. After about six
weeks I had a visit from a number of dockers, straight up from
the Wharf Tavern, proposing that I close down the Bingo. The
reason for their concern was that when they came home on two
nights a week, their wives were out! I pointed out that I did not
think it unfair that their wives should get out of the house two
nights a week when they themselves were generally out seven
nights a week. Another depressing fact about the relationship
between dockers and their wives I learned was that, with few
exceptions, dockers' wives never knew what their husbands
were earning.

The men who ran the parish hall belonged to a small confraternity (see Appendix 2). This consisted of between fifteen and
twenty men who worked in the docks area either as supervisors

or warehouse men and all of them were teetotallers. They met once a week, dressed in formal choir attire and together recited the Little Office of Our Blessed Lady. Twenty years earlier Fr Larry Redmond had recognised and used to the full the potential of this confraternity. Larry was a priest in the mould of Don Bosco. He regarded his mission as being to boys and men. He was assisted by the confraternity to run St Mary's Boys Club, which had been founded by a group of busmen and was re-organised by Larry. The members of the confraternity, in addition, ran an underage soccer league, acted as prefects in the Men's Sodality and helped in every other way required in the parish. The results of Larry's zealous curacy in East Wall were evident more than twenty years after he had been transferred elsewhere.

When residing in East Wall, one tended to have considerable sympathy for dockers. Theirs was a hard life. The work was exhausting, back-breaking and had to be done in all weathers. It had no fixed hours. They worked on a ship until it was 'cleared'. In addition, the docks and the Seamen's Union were controlled by a small group of families and cliques. The docker had to rise very early each morning and report to an assembly point. There he might or might not be called to work. Whether he was or not often had little connection with the justice of his claim to be given an opportunity to work on that day.

In spite of the updating of equipment in the docks, some extraordinary work practices were allowed to continue. The men worked in gangs of three, five or seven. In the gang of five, very often only four were required, in that of seven only five. Yet they were fitted out with ghost members: dockers not even physically present but who were paid as if they were. Another abuse arose from overtime. The dockers were credited with double time on Saturday and treble time on Sunday. The result was that very often an adequate number of dockers would not be available for duty on Monday, Tuesday, Wednesday or Thursday, but there would be no shortage of them on Friday, Saturday or especially Sunday! The authorities turned a Nelson eye to these and other practices, as in return those who ran the docks ensured that the level of pilfering in the area never rose above insignificant levels. When residing in East Wall for some time, one came to regard such activities in the docks not so much as corruption as what went on in the 'real world'. However, even then there was uncertainty as to how long this 'real world' would continue. Already shipping companies, haulage operators and other users of the port were engaging in discussions with the Port and Docks Board on fundamental changes, notably the introduction of container traffic, which would have most serious, long term implications for the dockers.

My predecessor, Fr Cronan Byrne, had been patron of East Wall United, a junior soccer club. The committee invited me to succeed him which I gladly did. It was the leading junior club in the country. In my years as patron, the club won the FAI Junior Cup twice. Most of the players worked on the docks.

I recall that it was on the Sunday as I was sitting on the stand in Dalymount Park enjoying the final of the Junior Cup that I first learned about the details of 'ghosting' on the docks. One of our wingers, Brendan Mooney, had scored what proved to be the winning goal. A member of the committee next to me said that this was a very good day for Brendan. Besides playing 'a blinder' for the club, he was at the same time, as a 'ghost', earning treble time down in the docks! Quite a number of the sons and nephews of the team members of the East Wall AFC were later well-known players in the League of Ireland.

Excessive drinking was the tragedy of the docker's life. The docker was practically predestined to be a heavy drinker. The strategically placed pubs around the docks area, peer pressure, very often the payment of wages in pubs, periods of time when the dockers were not required but had to be on call and not too far from the docks – all tended to make the pub the centre of the docker's life. The pub provided warmth, comfort, above all company and an escape from the harsh conditions of the docks. However a high price had to be paid for this. Although earning high wages, relative to other manual workers, all too many of the dockers spent the bulk of their earnings on drink and left themselves and their families impoverished.

I recall being immensely saddened on one occasion when coming face to face with this fact. The centre forward and star of East Wall United was a docker. A handsome, pleasant, six-footer, he was in his early thirties. He had developed a serious drink problem. For a few seasons he had played in the League of Ireland with different clubs. While his football skill ensured success at that level, the clubs had to drop him because of indiscipline and lack of fitness arising from his drinking. During the course of my pastoral visitation, I called on his family and home. It consisted of a young waif-like wife, two small children and just one large room. I was reminded of the Dublin tenements at the turn of the century.

The food centre in St Mary's Road I had to supervise had been established under the auspices of the Catholic Social Service Conference in 1942 and continued until 1975. (For more on this and other food centres, see *Handbook of the Catholic Social Service Conference* (Dublin 1945) and Mary Purcell, *50 years of the Catholic Social Service Conference: a brief history* (Dublin 1991).) The costs involved in running it were met by the conference with the aid of a very small grant from Dublin Corporation. The main aim of the centre was to ensure that the young mothers of the district were provided each day with at least one nourishing meal of meat, vegetables and potatoes, a rice or tapioca pudding and a cup of tea. Food parcels were also distributed from the centre to the elderly and the house bound. It was open every day except Sunday. Sister Vincent Brooks of the Daughters of Charity of St Vincent de Paul, who resided in their convent in William Street, came over each morning and ran it with a few local helpers. The number of those attending varied, but generally was between eighty and one hundred. Sister Vincent's commitment to the work was total. She availed of every opportunity on feast days and other occasions to provide little luxuries for the women, whose affection and reverence for her was at times quite moving.

My role was to look after the administration and the accounts of the centre. I called in to see Sister and her guests a few times each week. Sister charged those who came to the centre and who could afford it one shilling per meal. However, she never refused to serve anyone who turned up, whether they paid or not. Sometimes she would have to call on me to police the centre. From time to time the numbers of dockers using the centre could result in some of the young mothers for whom it was primarily intended not being catered for. These dockers would be in receipt of large wages but spent only a minimum on food and the rest on drink. When the problem became acute, Sister would call on me for help.

My role would be to explain to these dockers the purpose of the food centre and to insist and ensure that they waited until the young mothers had been served. I also would insist on them paying the shilling which they never did when Sister was on her own. I hated this chore but felt it had to be done. It was not without its pressures. After one of these episodes I had a delegation of three dockers call on me. They advised me in the clearest terms not to be interfering down at the food centre. I told them that come what may I intended to do my job. Moreover I told them that if there was any thuggery around the presbytery or the food centre I would create an unholy fuss and that at best I would ensure that no docker would henceforth be fed at the food centre and that at worst I would do my best to have it closed.

The chaplaincy which gave me most satisfaction was that of the Women's Sodality. Externally at least it was very successful, not least owing to an excellent team of prefects. There was always a good turnout at the monthly meeting and general communion on the following Sunday. To make it attractive, the small group who helped me to run it decided to make it the focus of socials in the parish. We also organised occasional excursions to Glendalough, Skerries, Butlins, etc.

In the space of two years the Sodality organised three pilgrimages, one to Rome, another to Lourdes, and the third to Rome, Loreto, Assisi and San Giovanni Rotundo. Máiréad Doyle was the inspiration of the third pilgrimage, the main aim of

which was to visit Padre Pio in San Giovanni Rotundo, in southern Italy. At that time Máiréad had become aware of the devotion to Padre Pio and was one of those asked to spread it in
Ireland. This she did with characteristic enthusiasm. Eventually
she and Mrs Mona Hannafin became national figures in this
regard and I was delighted for them and all members of the
Padre Pio prayer groups throughout the country when the
Italian Capuchin was beatified in 1998.

The highlight of our third pilgrimage was the four days we
spent in San Giovanni Rotundo. In 1966 there was not much to
be seen in that tiny village on a rocky hillside. A very large,
ultra-modern hospital seemed completely out of place. It had
been built for the poor of the region by Padre Pio with donations
from American devotees who had heard of him from GIs serving in Europe after World War II. The Capuchin monastery and
chapel were quite small, in keeping with the size of the village.
Padre Pio celebrated Mass each morning at 5. However to have
any opportunity to get into the chapel one had to arrive before
4.30. His Mass was simple, prayerful and brief, not more than
twenty minutes. Even then he was infirm and he was assisted by
two confreres. His large eyes were the main feature of his handsome face and his rapt attention left one in no doubt as to his
conviction of what he was about.

Padre Pio spent most of each day, except Sunday, hearing
confessions. Although no flowers were to be seen, I was surprised to find a strong smell of roses in the room where he sat.
When confessing, I noticed that the stigmata had stained the
bandage on his hands, joined in prayer. Close up, his face was
almost radiant. We were all impressed by our visit to San
Giovanni Rotundo and grateful to Máiréad for persuading us to
make it.

During my second year in East wall, I became a close friend
of Mr Jack Lynch. Mr Lynch, I never addressed him in any other
way, was the father of my classmate Fr Jack Lynch. I knew Mr
Lynch before coming to East wall, as Jack and I, when students
in Clonliffe, spent some of one summer holiday in each other's

homes. Mr Lynch, a Dublin city bus driver, was a perfect gentle-man. Sadly in 1966 he had a major operation for cancer and had to take early retirement. During his long convalescence and retirement, he read a great deal and had a preference for books on serious subjects. At the time I was reading very widely also. We were both fortunate in having excellent branches of Dublin City Libraries nearby at Charleville Mall and Marino. Most afternoons, weather permitting, I would call on Mr Lynch and we would enjoy a walk in Fairview Park and a discussion of what we were reading. Happily Mr Lynch had a much longer retirement than was initially anticipated.

When I was in East Wall the nation celebrated the fiftieth anniversary of the Easter Rising. I was very pleased that due honour was paid to those who took part in that heroic event. However, apart from a few very committed Republican families and a number of families who had settled in the district after they had fled from Northern Ireland during the anti-Catholic pogroms of the 1920s and the clearing of Catholics out of the Harland and Wolf shipyard, there was not much enthusiasm throughout the parish for the celebrations. RTE dramatised a number of the historical events. These were good but I felt they should have been better. It seemed to me that some of our well-known actors who had roles in these presentations had not appreciated the difference between acting on stage for a live audience and acting/speaking to a TV camera.

Fr Fred Hooke, the parish priest in East Wall, was a small man and both good-humoured and pious. He had been a priest in the Holy Ghost Missionary Order but had a breakdown in health. After recovering he served as a curate for many years in the parish of Lucan. Then with the help of his brother, a Dublin diocesan priest, he managed to be incardinated into the archdio-cese. This may have left him with a feeling of insecurity. At any rate he kept very much to himself and when occasionally out and about in the parish he met somebody he reacted almost like a rabbit surprised outside its burrow. He was a lively preacher and used a lot of phrases which could be found in Sean

O'Casey's plays. Like O'Casey, he picked up these listening to the conversation of the local people. Fred Hooke was always kind and courteous and was well-liked by all the priests who served with him.

CHAPTER 8

Our Lady of Good Counsel, Mourne Road, Drimnagh 1967-1970

In the summer changes of 1967 I was transferred to a curacy in the parish of Our Lady of Good Counsel, in Drimnagh. The parish was generally known as Mourne Road from the wide road which ran diagonally through the parish. It was constituted in 1942 from Terenure and Dolphin's Barn parishes. In 1967 it had just under 30,000 parishioners, a parish priest, six curates and a secondary school chaplain. When I arrived in Mourne Road it was a vibrant parish with a vibrant staff.

Mourne Road was one of a number of very large parishes which Archbishop John Charles McQuaid had established with remarkable foresight in the 1940s, 1950s and 1960s. From the late 1930s to the early 1960s Dublin Corporation was engaged in extensive building and re-housing programmes on the outskirts of the city: at Artane, Ballyfermot, Cabra, Coolock, Crumlin, Donnycarney, Drimnagh, Finglas, Larkhill, Marino and Raheny. The archbishop assigned some of his most able and dedicated priests to these areas so that by their presence and service they would mould the residents into viable communities which could later be formally established as parishes. These priests generally began by ensuring the establishment of the schools required in the area. Then with a temporary church or in a school hall they would, mainly through their Sunday Masses and other services, build up a consciousness among the residents of their belonging to, and being part of, a parish community. The working together of the priests and people to this end and positive results from their efforts created an exceptional bond between them and a crusading-type spirit which remained in these parishes for at least a generation.

The archbishop was particularly successful in persuading various female religious orders to take responsibility for the education of the girls and young women in these areas. As a result of their dedicated teaching and that of their lay colleagues, the women in these emerging parishes became a 'Faith people', that is, they had a grasp of their religion matching their general academic development and were imbued with Christian values. The teaching of religion in the Boys' School was equally successful, but it was the crucial influence of the Nuns' past pupils in their homes and the parish which set the Christian and upwardly mobile tone in these areas. In Mourne Road it was the Sisters of Mercy who were the leaders of this traditionally Christian building up of community.

Fr Dan Delany who served as parish priest in Mourne Road from 1949 to 1960 was an outstanding pastor. Years after his death parishioners spoke of him with great affection and appreciation. With a larger than life personality, he was intensely loyal to, and prepared to spend himself for, his people, but he also reproved them when the occasion demanded it. He urged the people to take a pride in themselves and their parish. They did and cherished him for urging them to do so.

To have a church of which the people would be proud Dan, mainly because of the extensive use of decorative marble, went far beyond the budget proposed by the diocesan authorities. This he did in spite of the archbishop and to his considerable annoyance. In due course the archbishop came to bless the new church, replete with marble. Tight-lipped, he said not a word. But, as he and Dan left the church after the blessing, he remarked: 'Marble is very cold, Father.'

Fr Dan was succeeded by Fr Jamesie Doyle. He had been parish priest of St Audeon's in the Liberties. The responsibility of Mourne Road weighed heavily on him, not least because he suffered a great deal from asthma and was frequently ill. He offered the 9 o'clock Mass every Sunday for the people of the parish, celebrated a private Mass at the same time each weekday, was an excellent confessor and presided at meetings of the parish staff. The state of his health and the enthusiastic commitment of his staff to their pastoral duties did not leave him room to do much more than that.

Jamesie had a good, self-deprecating sense of humour. On one occasion at a meeting of the priests he told us how he had decided to concentrate on one aspect of pastoral activity, namely, to visit and spend some time with every bereaved family in the parish. The first death which occurred after he had made this decision was in a home directly opposite his parochial house on the quite narrow Sperrin Road. He went across to the house in the gloom of a November evening, mumbled who he was and was invited into a room full of people drinking glasses of stout. He soon had a drink put in front of him. After some forced conversation and staying long enough to drink half the glass of stout he stood up and excused himself. The lady of the house then addressed those in the room saying: 'Fr Doyle of Mount Argus has to leave now!'

As was customary at the time, after receiving my transfer on a Monday morning I reported for the session of confessions in my new parish on the following Saturday evening. In the meantime I had presented myself to my new parish priest. He was affable and welcoming and told me he was particularly eager that I should visit the families in my district. I assured him that at the end of three months I would have called on all the houses in my district. In the event it took me four months to get round to all 870 of them.

There was a good tradition of pastoral visitation in the archdiocese and I soon realised how important and useful it was. In all my curacies I had a visiting card printed and once a year called on every house in my area of responsibility. In most of my curacies I inherited a *Liber Status Animarum* from my predecessor. This was a register printed according to the requirements of Canon Law. Each priest brought this on visitation and recorded or updated the names, dates of birth, sacraments received, schools attended and other relevant information on parents and children. The title of the register, literally, 'The book of the State of Souls' indicated that the priest's main role was to be concerned with the eternal salvation of parishioners rather than being the mere provider of social services.

In part of my district which contained the poorest families in the parish there was a large number of very vulnerable and under-privileged families. The main reason for this was a decision by Dublin Corporation some years earlier to close Keogh Square in Inchicore after a prolonged, public outcry about the living conditions there. This had been a former British army barracks and for decades the Corporation had 'dumped' into it its most difficult and incorrigible tenants. They were re-housed in surrounding areas, including Drimnagh. The men folk in these families were unemployed and, to be honest, unemployable. An alarmingly high proportion of the teenagers, especially the sons, in these families attended St Loman's Psychiatric Hospital.

During my pastoral visitation in Mourne Road I came across the 'drug problem' for the first time. Prior to this my only awareness of drug abuse was the occasional reference to it in a Hollywood film. On more occasions than I care to remember I would, during the course of visitation in the early afternoon, be invited into the kitchen by a mother who would tearfully tell me that one of her sons had fallen into bad company and had become 'involved in drugs'. She would share with me the anxiety and heartache of herself and the other members of the family with this son being out all night, practically every night, in search of drugs and the money to pay for them. On a number of occasions a mother brought me into the small front room, used as a parlour, and there laid out like a corpse in his clothes would be the son, comatose, the only sign of life his eyes following us. The drug addicts were responsible for most of the wanton destruction which blighted that neighbourhood. I always had immense sympathy for the decent families who suffered such disruption and pain from members who had got themselves hooked on drug-taking. For the addicts themselves I found it very difficult at times to have sympathy.

One of my specific duties in the parish was to act as chaplain to the senior classes in the Boys' Primary School. This had 2,500 pupils and an outstanding principal, John B. Supple, who was president of the national St Joseph's Young Priests' Society from 1963 to 1969. There were some other excellent teachers on the staff, including Tom Gilmore who served for many years on the executive of the INTO. For its size and inclusivity, the standard of discipline and orderly conduct maintained in the school was remarkable. Each week I visited the school and taught religious knowledge for a period in one of the classes and managed to visit every class once each school term.

I also had responsibility for the altar-boys. These I was bequeathed by Fr Tommy Randles. Tommy had put a lot of effort into developing an excellent *esprit de corps* among them and I simply followed the procedures he had put in place. There were over eighty altar boys, about 50 juniors and 30 seniors. I met the juniors every Tuesday afternoon and the seniors every Thursday for half-an-hour. There was no shortage of recruits and the seniors took turns in training them. My role was to supervise and prepare the weekly list providing two servers for each of the seven Masses celebrated in the parish each day and for the frequent Nuptial Masses. The youngsters were delightful: eager, lively and sharp-witted. A number of them were later ordained, including Frs Joe Connolly and Martin and Tom Noone.

In coping with the altar boys I had the assistance of Tom Barrett, the unsung hero of Mourne Road parish. A native of Cork city, at an early age he had begun his early working life in a car factory at Cowley, near Oxford. After many years he returned home to Ireland and shortly afterwards was appointed by Fr Dan Delany as his sacristan.

Tom loved his job and it showed. Always smiling and in good humour, it was a tonic to meet him at any time during the day. Highly intelligent and very competent, he supervised and completed the paperwork associated with the registration of marriages and baptisms. He prepared an index of the marriages and baptisms in the parish and so was able to issue certificates of these almost as quickly as people verbally requested them. He was particularly skilled in dealing with difficult persons and awkward situations. Tom had a great affection for all 'my priests', as he called us, and it was reciprocated.

One aspect of my association with the altar-boys which I particularly enjoyed was taking them on their frequent outings. Tom Barrett presided over the altar-boys' fund. The youngsters lodged in this the tips they received for serving at Nuptial Masses. This, with a subsidy from the parish, financed the outings. In the summer we went to Red Island in Skerries, Butlins in Mosney and the beach in Portmarnock.

Each winter we went to a few films. The youngsters decided what films we went to and on most occasions they chose what was suitable. I recall their rapt attention at the excitement and tension of 'Grand Prix', a film crafted around Formula One car racing.

I do not have a happy recollection of 'Dr Zhivago'. This splendid film had too many romantic interludes for them. David Lean's obsession with the stunning beauty of the Russian steppes in spring, obvious in long, lingering camera takes, went over their heads. Soon they were bored, then restless and eventually their chattering rose to a crescendo. They had bought so many sweets in the cinema *foyer* that they were throwing them at each other. The management switched on the lights on three occasions in unsuccessful attempts to quell the racket.

I was helpless to do anything about it. On that occasion Tom Barrett who usually accompanied me on the outings – he was as fond of the altar-boys as he was of his priests – was not with me. And I was also without my excellent head altar-boy, Gerry MacDonald. I suspected that a few of the wilder spirits were intent on getting their own back on me for the strict discipline I insisted on at our weekly meetings. I stayed in my seat and continued to stare at the screen. On the way out with my eighty or so miscreants I avoided looking at the other patrons who were exceedingly annoyed. At our next meeting, tongue-in-cheek, I told them that they had disgraced me and themselves.

Unfortunately through my association with the altar boys I had a little *contre temps* with the parish priest. He celebrated Mass every morning at 9 and, as for the other priests' Masses, I provided two different altar-boys to serve it each week. Fr Doyle was a perfectionist as far as liturgy was concerned. Among priests we have an anecdote which runs: 'What is the difference between a terrorist and a liturgist?' Answer: 'You can negotiate with a terrorist.' It has more than a grain of truth.

In the sacristy after Mass the parish priest invariably pointed out to the youngsters the mistakes they had made either in the responses or their actions. This was quite helpful and useful. But then during the Mass he dismissed a few who were particularly inept and sent them back tearfully to the sacristy. I felt I could not ignore this and for a month I did not appoint anyone to serve his Mass. Eventually he rang me and I told him that the youngsters were unwilling to serve his Mass, as he was too much of a perfectionist. After a week I resumed assigning the altar boys to his Mass and thereafter he appreciated having two willing youngsters to serve his Mass, albeit imperfectly.

Another of my tasks in Mourne Road was acting as chaplain to the St Vincent de Paul Society. There were three conferences. Two met on one night and the third on a separate night. I managed to spend at least a half-hour at each of the meetings each week. Members of the conference had plenty to do. Jim Ward, a senior civil servant in the Department of Posts and Telegraphs, was president of the senior conference. Apart from his St Vincent de Paul activities, he spent most of his free time helping young men in the area into jobs.

Vinnie Byrne was in Jim's conference. He had been a member of Michael Collins' legendary 'Squad'. Jim always addressed Vinnie jokingly as the 'captain', a reference to his rank in the IRA. Vinnie was tight-lipped but in a one to one situation he could be fascinating in recalling his exploits.

For the three years I was in Mourne Road, with a small committee of Vincent de Paul members I organised an annual Charity Concert to raise funds for the Society. Because the members of the

committee were at work all day, it fell to me to personally canvass the various artists and persuade them to take part in it.
From my time in East Wall I was able to get my friend, Jimmy
Banks, the accomplished pianist, and through him Tommy Ellis
and Peter Brady. This combo provided the musical link-up at
the three concerts. Fr Mick Cleary acted as MC. I was also able to
get Johnny McEvoy, then making a name for himself, and Maxi,
Dick and Twink.

There were others but the star of the show was always local
girl, Patricia Cahill. A talented singer and a beautiful girl, she
had a marvellous repertoire of Irish songs and was very popular. She was and remained ever a credit to her family, friends
and the parish. I was generally disappointed by the income gen-
erated by these concerts. While we had little difficulty in 'selling
the house', our overheads were considerable mainly because all
the performing artists, with the exception of Mick Cleary and
Patricia Cahill, insisted on their full professional fees.

It was comparatively easy to put on a show in Mourne Road.
A well-equipped hall formed part of the parish plant. There was
a flourishing musical society, of which Fr Johnnie Casey was the
founder and inspiration. Mrs Jennie McKeown Ryan, the parish
organist and choir mistress, and most of the choir formed the
backbone of the society. Each year Johnnie and the secretary of
the Musical Society, Nora O'Neill, had the society present a popular musical for about a week which matched in professionalism
and quality the shows of the R & R. While most of the cast would
be local talent, one or two of the principal roles would be sung
by well-known professionals from abroad.

Another chore which I had in Mourne Road was the 'Poor
Box'. I regarded it as such, seeing that it had associations with
Judas Iscariot. Looking after the 'Poor Box' meant counting the
generous and numerous offerings deposited in it and then issu-
ing grants from it on request to one or other of my colleagues.
This occurred when they were faced with the need to come to
the rescue of someone in their district who could not be helped
financially in the usual way by the St Vincent de Paul Society or
otherwise.

About a year after arriving in Drimnagh I heard of a Meals on Wheels service in Crumlin. It was run by the Irish Sisters of Charity. I went up to see it and went out on the delivery run on a few occasions. The Sisters and their helpers delivered about twenty two-course lunches to house-bound three days a week. The Sisters received a small grant to this end from the Eastern Health Board.

I was aware that there was a need for such a service in Drimnagh and contacted Fred O'Donoghue, who organised and sponsored such services for the Eastern Health Board. Fred guaranteed to pay for meals if I could arrange to provide them and deliver them. When I requested the Sister, a Daughter of Charity, who was in charge of the kitchen in Our Lady's Hospital for Sick Children to provide twenty or thirty extra meals each day she readily agreed to do so. The Sisters who were engaged in the Meals on Wheels service in Crumlin advised me to start by delivering just twice weekly. I told them that from the outset I would try to deliver daily, as if the people really needed meals on two days a week they needed them every other day also. I also had some difficulty in persuading Fred to subsidise meals every day but he eventually agreed to the proposal. The equipment, containers, dishes, etc., had to be imported from England. After waiting impatiently for two months while the Eastern Health Board debated whether they could cover the expenditure on them I paid for them from parish funds.

In the meantime I selected a small committee of bright, young women to run the project and set about getting 70 volunteer drivers and 70 volunteer servers. My intention was that people would be called upon to help only once every eight weeks. Without a moment's reflection my five fellow-curates volunteered as drivers. With this information I called on the parish priest, told him of the proposed project and cleared it with him. I persuaded him to place his name on the list also as a driver. He was not too keen, as, he told me, at that time he was beginning to get nervous about driving. I told him that his name on the list was important to me, as it indicated he was fully supportive of the project and that, if he was not able to drive on any occasion, I would take his place.

Almost all the people I canvassed agreed to help. I signed up the local TDs as drivers: Joe Dowling (Fianna Fáil), John O'Connell (Labour) and Jimmy O'Keeffe (Fine Gael). Seán Dunne (Labour) had just died at that time. Alderman Lauri Corcoran led a few other Dublin Corporation members on to my list. Lauri was already very active in the parish, in particular in helping to run the flourishing Don Bosco Boys Club.

The priests and the Vincent de Paul conferences provided me with names for the Meals on Wheels list. The small committee met monthly and drew up the monthly schedule. In the early stages they also went out with those doing the delivery for the first time. Joe Kirley, a professional photographer and father of the secretary of the committee, and myself stood by in the event of a driver failing to turn up. However, it was only very seldom that a hitch occurred, as each driver and server received a full list of their schedules for the month with their phone numbers and were requested to make whatever interchange they required themselves. Once we got started we delivered a two-course lunch to about 30 house-bound persons every day of the year.

With regard to the Meals on Wheels service I recall feeling rather smug one Christmas eve morning. I answered the door bell to a man who told me he was a member of the St Vincent de Paul committee which organised the Christmas dinner at the Mansion House and asked me if there were any elderly people on their own or house-bound persons from the parish who wished to attend. I grandly informed him that all our house-bound would have their Christmas dinner delivered to their homes, just as they had their dinners delivered every other day of the year.

Encouraged by the degree to which people were prepared to help with the Meals on Wheels project I decided to do something about another need which I had noted in the district. Many retired workers from Guinness' Brewery and other businesses resided in the area. One noticed them walking or sitting on benches in the green spaces, even on bitterly cold days. There was no library or suitable meeting room within a reasonable distance where they could read a newspaper or relax.

Off Curlew Road a large building stood idle. It had been built some twenty years earlier as part of the campaign against TB. A local man acted as caretaker, opened and closed it every day and kept it heated in damp and cold weather. I was given permission by the Eastern Health Board to use a large room in it. With a small committee of ladies I opened the Pope John XXIII Club for retired men, complete with membership cards. Soon most of the retired Guinness workers and other local elderly men relaxed in it after attending, as most of them did, the daily 10 o'clock Mass. The Guinness Company generously delivered a case of stout each week and I was also successful in having the daily news-papers delivered free each day. Later we added a little library.

After a few months the very active ladies committee arranged to have a Women's Club in the premises in the after-noons. The women, of course, were provided with tea and biscuits – not a bottle of stout!

To ensure access to these and other services I had a card printed giving the name and phone number of the key person in each of them. I distributed about 80 of these to everyone in the parish active in the voluntary social services.

With the people in Drimnagh so active in a wide range of cultural, educational and social activities an article appeared in the *Irish Times* in March 1970 which ignored this aspect of 'Dublin South-West'. The fifth year girls in Good Counsel Secondary School were angry on reading this negative, unfair and mean-spirited description of their parish and district. Through the Sister who taught them English, they invited me to visit their class to discuss the article. Together we drafted a detailed reply which was published in the *Irish Times*.

In the late spring of 1970 the archbishop came to confer the sacrament of confirmation in the parish. In preparation for his arrival the six cars in front of the double-presbytery were dis-cretely parked elsewhere to the amusement of our neighbours. This practice was known as 'not pulling the cat's tail'.

There was in the archdiocese a consensus that it was inappropriate, in general, for priests to be attached to wealth or the trappings of wealth and in particular for young priests to be the owners of new expensive and flashy cars. At the time cars were not very plentiful and were still associated with people who were well-off. Thus, in effect, in diocesan terms the cars were regarded as a luxury which one had and used if required for one's work. If for health reasons or the nature of the parish a car was necessary a priest wrote to the archbishop for permission to buy one and usually received an affirmative reply by return of post. However, a certain ambiguity was left hanging as to what was to happen in the event of receiving a subsequent appointment where a car was not essential. In the event, most of the priests kept their cars and were not eager that the issue should be clarified, hence the reluctance to confront the archbishop with this fact.

The archbishop was not eager to confront the issue either. I recall an incident which occurred about 1962 which involved my friend, Fr Eamon MacSweeney. At the time Eamon was chaplain to Loughlinstown Hospital. He was a rather blithe spirit, received some money from his family and had a passion for cars. The more elegant they were, the better he liked them. Eamon never bothered to apply for permission to purchase a car, although he would have been entitled to one, as he resided a good distance from the hospital where he had a very early daily Mass and had other duties around the parish. In any case the archbishop traded in his car, a distinctive, upmarket Citroen for a new model. Eamon bought it and, as the archbishop also resided in the Ballybrack-Killiney area, he and Eamon occasionally passed each other on the road. Eventually Eamon nearly collided with the archbishop's car at a crossroads. A few days later, in a typical example of his sardonic humour, the archbishop sent a verbal message to Eamon which ran: 'The archbishop hopes you are taking good care of his car!'

Apart from conferring confirmation in Mourne Road the archbishop conducted a parish visitation. The original Greek from which the word bishop is derived literally means an overseer. John Charles took this aspect of his office very seriously. He would cast a sharp, penetrating eye around any church or other building he entered. During a parish visitation he checked the parish registers. If he discovered an entry with a biro, this could lead to a lecture on its unsuitability for important records which were meant to last.

Parish visitation also involved an interview with each of the priests on the staff. He began with the parish priest and worked down according to seniority. It was customary for each of us to bring along our *Liber Status Animarum*, as it was known he was particularly eager that priests should remain close to the people by regular house visitation. I was looking forward to having a chat with him, something I never had before then or subsequently. Indeed, I met him on only a handful of occasions. I imparted a blessing to him after he ordained me, and kissed his ring at a meeting of priest-teachers in archbishop's house and at a few confirmation ceremonies when he did not stay on for the confirmation dinner.

At Mourne Road the archbishop remained for the confirmation dinner. His presence did not in any way detract from its enjoyment by the rest of us. The dinner followed the pattern which I had heard characterised such occasions. A remarkably abstemious person, while the rest of those at table would be tucking in to a gargantuan meal, he would be fiddling with his fork with a piece of boiled chicken, followed by a small portion of steamed rice. It was *de riguere* to pour out his cup of tea at the end of the meal from an earthenware teapot. At some confirmation dinner he had made a fuss when it had been served from a silver tea-set and tea-pot. For the most part the parish priest and senior curate would occupy him in conversation about banalities. However, a topic of general and current interest would now and then arise and capture the attention of the table. John Charles would then pronounce in magisterial fashion on the topic or if he was not able to do that he would reveal a generally unknown and startling piece of information about it.

Before the dinner the archbishop conducted the brief interviews with the priests in the parochial house. I had no sooner sat
down facing him when he told me that the parish priest had
found my work unsatisfactory. I asked him what did he mean.
He replied that I had been late for helping to distribute communion and into my confessional on the occasion of the hearing of
confessions. I replied that that was not only untrue but that it
was ridiculous. Continuing, I pointed out that the distribution of
communion took about five minutes and I had never missed
that duty, and like all the other staff members I entered my confessional at five minutes past seven every Saturday night for the
7 to 9.30 session. I was particularly annoyed by this last charge,
as my confessional was the first as one entered the church and I
was never other than busy throughout the entire 7 to 9.30 session,
as I was also each Saturday during a session from 11 to 12.

Next he enquired if I had visited the families in my district. I
replied that I had. He appeared to doubt my word and I told him
I resented that. He ended the interview. Before leaving I told
him I wished to resume the interview when he had seen the rest
of the priests and that I was determined with the independent
evidence of any of my colleagues to show how ridiculous the
charges made against me were. Unfortunately we were both angry
at this stage. Very sensibly Monsignor Liam Martin persuaded me
not to go in to see him when the interviews had concluded. I sat at
the other end of the table from the archbishop at the subsequent
confirmation dinner!

Apart from myself, I blamed the parish priest not the archbishop for this nonsense. I never had anything but the highest
regard and respect for John Charles McQuaid. He was an exemplary priest and in retrospect I would rate him the outstanding
Irish bishop of his generation. He had qualities I greatly admire:
moral courage, integrity and loyalty. His commitment to the
material as well as spiritual well-being of the people of the archdiocese was constant. The poor, the weak, the marginalised
were his special concern and he prided himself in being their
champion. A most able and talented person, his forte was his

administrative skill and his capacity for work. The amount of work which he got through was awesome.

The archbishop's secretaries were equally hard-working. It will never be known how much the archdiocese owes to Frs John Fitzpatrick, Ardle MacMahon, Chris Mangan, Liam Martin, Michael O'Connell and Des Williams who at various times were his secretaries. Theirs was a 24 hour a day job. They resided with him in a house in Killiney which had been presented to the archdiocese for his use. The house was made available by the archbishop's step-brother, Matt. He was very popular with his peers in the business community of the city and he and a number of his associates donated the £3,000 required to purchase the house. Soon after the archbishop moved into it and changed its name from 'Ashhurst' to 'Notre Dame du Bois', a priest of the archdiocese, when showing the head of an American mega company around Killiney, decided to take a look at the archbishop's new residence. As he and his US visitor viewed the fine home and extensive well-kept grounds, the priest said: 'The archbishop resides here with his secretaries.' To which the visitor replied: 'Gee, I'd say they're cute.'

With regard to personality John Charles was not naturally gifted. He was exceedingly sensitive, shy and reserved. This, it seemed to me, left him with a sense of insecurity which he compensated for by adopting a headmasterly and at times even over-bearing attitude to fellow adults. In any case it is arguable that anyone, who has been a teacher or especially a headmaster, as John Charles was, tends to retain some of the characteristics associated with these roles. This and his mannerisms were easy to mimic and were brilliantly exploited by Fr Mick Cooney who for years entertained his colleagues with his act. John Charles was aware of this and on one occasion came unexpectedly on Mick in the middle of his performance in a characteristic pose with one shoulder raised above the other. As he passed he said: 'Wrong shoulder, Father.'

I gave my colleagues a word for word account of my interview with the archbishop. They were all agreed that I could expect a transfer very soon out of Mourne Road. Light-heartedly they began to speculate as to where I might end up. There was a general consensus that it would be a fair distance from archbishop's house. Sure enough three weeks later my change arrived. It was to St Patrick's, Monkstown, then one of the most desirable curacies in the archdiocese.

I was pleasantly surprised, as I had not, in the meantime, bothered to make representations to anyone about the matter. My colleagues figured out the situation as follows. On the one hand the archbishop had to move me because of my non-deferential attitude. On the other hand he had obviously gone a little deeper into the matter and the promotion he was giving me was as close as he could go to an admission that he had been misinformed and perhaps unjust.

In due course John Charles offered his resignation in 1970 on reaching 75 years of age. This he did in accordance with post-Vatican II regulations. His resignation was accepted at the end of 1971 and announced on 4 January 1972. I wrote congratulating him on his tireless work for the people of the archdiocese of Dublin and the inspiring example he gave to his priests. I received an immediate appreciative reply. About a year later I was disgusted to hear how after he had tendered his resignation in 1970 he was undermined from within, in a disloyal and underhand fashion, by persons who were determined to ensure who would succeed him.

Basic duties in Mourne Road parish were onerous. The church was full for Sunday Masses. At the late Masses people queued outside the doors to enter as the previous congregations left. Sessions in the confessional were always very heavy. One usually did about ten baptisms at a time. From my district I had to arrange and officiate at many marriages: in the summer about five a week and sometimes two on the same day. During my time in the parish the planned-giving was re-vamped. Fr Val Martin had responsibility for this across the parish but each of us helped him to this end in our own district.

Each priest had one night a week on duty. On most nights the priest on duty would get a call in the small hours. Apart from conferring the last rites the people used us to ensure that an ambulance would be alerted to take the seriously ill person to the hospital. There were a number of reasons for this. Few people had telephones and the public telephones would invariably be vandalised and out of order. Also for some reason or other the medical cover of the area was very unsatisfactory. In this last regard, however, there was at least one shining exception. Dr Barry Hooper, a local GP, was a tireless and much appreciated carer of the people of the district.

One could not anticipate what to expect on these night calls. On one occasion I found the young men in the house literally breaking the furniture from frustration at not being able to ring 999 and help for their critically ill father. After making the call from the presbytery I had to return to the house and spend almost two hours trying to get them all to calm down.

I never worked as hard in my life as I did during my three years in Mourne Road parish. Yet the usefulness and success of the work itself was an ample reward and the appreciation of the people, which was almost palpable was a bonus. Apart from the camaraderie of my colleagues and the many friends I had made in the parish, I knew I would miss 'Lark'. A very large, handsome Alsatian, he had been raised by Fr Pat Culhane from the time he was just a small pup. He was the presbytery mascot and I enjoyed taking him for a walk. I was very sorry leaving Mourne Road.

CHAPTER 9

St Patrick's, Monkstown
1970-1977

During the April changes of 1970 I arrived in St Patrick's parish in Monkstown and replaced Fr Bob Walsh who had been appointed parish priest of Saggart. Bob was a fellow-townsman from Listowel and a close friend.

He was a good raconteur, although one of his most interesting recollections was not a happy one. In April 1921 the IRA shot as a spy Sir Arthur Vicars and burned down his residence, Kilmorna House, three miles from Listowel. Two days later the crown forces selected the houses of four 'Sinn Feiners' in the town and decided as a reprisal to burn them down. Bob's father, John R. Walsh, was known to be a supporter of Sinn Féin and his was one of the residences and business premises listed for destruction. It happened that a week previously Bob's father, a former Kerry footballer, had presented Bob, aged eleven, with his first pair of football boots. When the British soldiers ordered the Walsh family out on the street before setting fire to their home, Bob, it seems, pleaded to no avail to be allowed to retrieve his football boots. Bob would end his description of the event by saying that he was able to forgive and forget everything the British did in Ireland except the burning of his football boots!

Bob and I were enthusiastic followers of the Kerry football team. In the National League season 1959-60 I accompanied him to all Kerry's away fixtures. Sometimes this involved travelling considerable distances. I vividly recall a trip to Carlow where Kerry, although All-Ireland champions, were held to a draw by an unfancied Carlow side in an exciting match.

My new parish was constituted in 1902 from Dún Laoghaire. In 1970 it consisted of some 7,500 parishioners, a parish priest and three curates. It was continually growing and a decision had been made to establish a new parish from it at Kill O' the Grange. Half of the new parish was to be provided by the Monkstown Farm district, the rest from a part of Foxrock parish and the extra houses being built in the area between Foxrock and Monkstown. Monkstown parish had three identifiable districts: upper middle class, middle class and working class. Notwithstanding this, there was surprisingly little snobbery in the parish.

It did not take me long to realise that Monkstown was a most agreeable appointment. For the first time I had a presbytery all to myself. This was also particularly gratifying to my housekeeper, Binnie Moran. She had been with me in East Wall and Mourne Road where she had to care for two and three priests respectively.

Fr Tom Barry, the parish priest, was a native of South County Kildare. He was a first cousin of Kevin Barry, a UCD medical student and member of the IRA who was captured after an ambush on British soldiers and hanged in November 1920. Tom never mentioned this. In fact he hardly ever mentioned anything. He was the most secretive person I ever met and kept such a low profile that he became almost invisible.

My new fellow-curates were Rex Hegarty and Hugh Daly. Both, like myself, had been drafted into the parish from very busy former appointments. Rex had spent about ten years in Ballyfermot where he had established a very successful parish branch of the Credit Union and Hugh had come from the then equally busy Westland Row parish.

In personality they were an interesting contrast. Rex was quiet, sensitive, retiring and very clever – he had obtained a first class honours MSc. Hugh was jolly, outgoing and full of fun. By the time I arrived they had well settled in to enjoy the change of tempo in their new parish and were in no hurry to be transferred elsewhere. At my first meeting with Rex and Hugh they indicated how much they were enjoying Monkstown. Rex then took me aside and said: 'In Monkstown we want no waves. We don't want those in archbishop's house to hear anything bad about Monkstown or anything good.'

In Monkstown there was the usual round of priestly duties: Masses, the provision of the sacraments, preaching, duty-days, etc. With my two colleagues we provided a 7.30, 8 and 10 Mass each weekday and two Masses each on Sundays and Holydays. As the junior curate I was always on the 7.30 Mass. This slight inconvenience was put into perspective for me on one occasion by Christy White. He was a bus conductor from Monkstown Farm who began each weekday by attending the 7.30 Mass. We became friends and I always drove him home after Mass, if the weather was inclement. On one December morning in my second year in the parish, as I was driving him home and complaining about the awful day it was, he put his hand on my shoulder and said: 'Fr, any day you can get up and have your breakfast is a wonderful day.' Sadly within a year Christy had died of a cancer that even appeared on his face.

Monkstown was exceptionally fortunate with regard to schools. At the Sacred Heart Convent the Sisters conducted a junior and a second level school for girls. At Monkstown CBC the Christian Brothers provided similar facilities for boys. Near St Patrick's church a small national school was being phased out and absorbed into the recently completed Blessed Oliver Plunkett School at Dunedin Park. This consisted of two schools which were juxtaposed: one for girls and one for boys. Most of its pupils were drawn from Monkstown Farm.

Tom Barry requested me to act as manager of Oliver Plunkett school on his behalf. This involved some paperwork, keeping in close touch with the principals and the supervision of a caretaker and four cleaners. The caretaker was not very effective and the school-building was frequently attacked by vandals. I quickly learned that it was essential to have broken windows replaced immediately.

A typical modern school building, it took a great deal of watching. I recall one particularly bad spate of window-breaking. Try as he did the caretaker could not catch the perpetrator. I decided to stake out the school myself and after several days caught a little mite, less than two feet high, red-handed. I took the toddler to his mother and sternly warned her that if he should do any more damage she would be paying for it. As the school was new, apart from vandalism, the supervision of its maintenance was not too burdensome.

As well as acting as manager of Oliver Plunkett school I was also chaplain to the girls' section of it. Rex Hegarty was chaplain to the boys' section. As was my practice I taught religion for a period in a different class each week. The standard of teaching throughout the girls' school was exceptional, none more so than in the class of Mrs Nell McLoughlin. Sheila Forde and Paddy Cahill, father of the sports journalist Des, were the respective principals, both of whom were good friends of mine.

Responsibility for the school included supervision of the school hall. At the time attempts, initiated by Fr Larry Redmond, were being made to establish a viable community centre at Monkstown House. However most of the social activity in the parish was still centred in the Oliver Plunket school hall which a small committee helped to run. We ran bingo on two nights a week. This should have been a good source of funds for the parish. After most sessions I generally returned home feeling frustrated. The caller, a mercurial character, in the excitement of the moment would so raise the level of some of the prizes and the 'snow ball' that our entire takings at the door would be dissipated. However, even when just breaking even, I felt that the bingo sessions were important such was the pleasure they gave to those who patronised them.

Teenage dancing created most problems with regard to the running of the hall. At one stage we had one every Sunday night and for a time they were particularly successful. Before agreeing to sanction them the hall committee insisted: (1) that they were supervised by a parents' committee, (2) that all those attending have membership cards and (3) that the dances be ended at 11.30 pm.

After seven or eight months the parents handed over the super-vision of the teenage dance to a committee of the youngsters themselves. Within a short time there were problems. Every Monday morning when I visited the school the exceedingly tol-erant principals would have to draw my attention to the mess left from the night before in and around the toilets. Then there was a serious problem about noise. The hall was on the edge of Monkstown Farm and in the immediate vicinity a number of elderly people and widows resided. For me that they should be inconvenienced was quite unacceptable. The teenagers were either unable or unwilling to end their social at 11.30. Without parental supervision they also raised the sound so that I and everyone else at Monkstown Avenue could hear it even at the other side of Dunedin Park. After a number of unsuccessful at-tempts to reason with the teenagers I had to close their social down. In this regard I met several delegations from them. They offered various reasons for keeping it going. One of the most curious, I recall, was that if they were not allowed to dance in the Oliver Plunkett hall they would then have to dance in the Knox Hall, a Protestant hall!

Tom Barry who had asked me to organise the teenage dancing was delighted with its closure. He was against it from the start but was intimidated into allowing it by a group of well-to-do parents who threatened to deliver a jointly signed letter to the archbishop protesting against his alleged lack of interest in the youth of the parish should he not promote a dance for teenagers. In the event, the burning interest of these parents in the youth or in-deed any other activities in the parish was limited to the rather short-lived involvement of their siblings in the teenage social.

In Monkstown I was once again chaplain to a parish branch of the St Vincent de Paul Society. I looked forward to the meet-ing every Tuesday night. It was generally an occasion of consid-erable merriment. There were a dozen members and Tony O'Brien who was half the age of most of them was the president. Roy Williams, brother of Fr Des, was the secretary. There were two Englishmen, the saintly Don Ross, a retired colonel of the Indian army, and Peter Bates, a businessman. Tony Ó hUadhaigh, head of the firm of solicitors of the same name, was always bubbling over with good humour and was a fund of good stories. The Falstafian Dick White, on his own, was capable of keeping the members of the conference chuckling during most of the meetings. In 1974 Maeve McMahon, then studying social science at UCD, joined the conference and her earnestness and enthusiasm impressed all of us.

Bunny O'Reilly was the grand old man of the conference – eventually he was to serve over fifty years as a member of the Society. Born with a silver spoon in his mouth, he was generally at the centre of every round of witty exchanges. Normally members visited those they are assisting in pairs but for some reason or other Bunny had to visit on one occasion on his own. A gentleman to his finger tips and always very proper in his conduct, I recall the amusement of the conference when he shame-facedly reported on his visit. It seems it was rather late when he called on a lady to deliver the weekly financial assistance she received. She refused to open the door, berated him and told him that the hour he attempted to visit was not an appropriate time for a gentleman to be calling on a respectable woman!

As well as their St Vincent de Paul work, Don Ross and Tony O'Brien, with others, established in Monkstown Community Centre a pre-school, play-group for children of less well-off parents. This first play-group in south Dublin was grant-aided by the Eastern Health Board but extra funding was required to maintain it. Most of the funds to this end were raised at that time by an annual sale of work. I recall introducing Eleanor Butler / Lady Wicklow when she formally opened the first sale of work with a characteristically gracious address.

I had little difficulty in setting up a Meals on Wheels project in Monkstown. The Sisters of Mercy in charge of the kitchen in Our Lady of Lourdes Hospital on Rochestown Avenue readily agreed to make 14 extra lunches available whenever required. The Eastern Health Board guaranteed to pay for them. I knew where to write for the necessary equipment. The committee I selected to run it with members from each section of the parish were most enthusiastic. It did not take too long with the help of the committee to persuade 40 persons to act as drivers and a similar number to act as servers. Such was the efficiency of our secretary, Noreen O'Sullivan, in preparing the monthly schedules and having us deliver them that our monthly committee meeting lasted only from ten to twenty minutes.

When underway we delivered 14 meals three days each week. There were some names on our list which would have been familiar to a previous generation: Mrs Bodkin, widow of a former director of the National Gallery of Ireland, Mrs Robinson, widow of the playwright Lennox Robinson, Mrs Smylie, widow of a former editor of the *Irish Times*, and Mrs Stockley, widow of a former professor in UCC. In Monkstown it was necessary to help the genteel as well as the ordinary poor. Almost half our recipients were members of the Church of Ireland. In late 1970, with Frank Gregan and Bill Tracey, I co-founded Carrickbrennan (Monkstown) Credit Union, the initial suggestion for this coming from Bill Tracey.

My area of responsibility in the parish was the 400 houses in the very compact Monkstown Farm together with Fitzgerald Park and Mountwood Flats. I quickly visited these and returned to re-vamp the planned-giving in the district. By the time I had finished 62 per cent of the householders in Monkstown Farm were contributing to the weekly collection. This was not surprising, as the collection was for the new church then being built and soon to be theirs.

In 1972 Kill O' the Grange parish was constituted, with Fr Andy Griffith as parish priest. I recall the marathon meeting of five and a half hours at which the financial and other details arising from the division of Monkstown parish were finalised. Owing to a protracted national strike of craftsmen, inflation and other unforeseeable circumstances, the beautiful new church cost about £280,000 instead of the agreed £200,000. Monkstown parish had already paid Con Creedon, the builder, £130,000. The meeting decided that Monkstown parish would take responsibility for £50,000 of the outstanding debt of £150,000. The meeting also decided that as Monkstown had three other schools Blessed Oliver Plunkett school should be incorporated into the new parish.

Hugh Daly was transferred into the new parish. Rex and I greatly missed him. He was ever an easy-going, cheerful and delightful companion. The easy-going atmosphere of Monkstown

affected all of us, not least Hugh. This was evident at a confirmation I vividly recall. Bishop Joe Carroll came to confer the sacrament. I was an admirer and had considerable regard for Joe
from the time I attended his Introductory Scripture class in
Clonliffe in 1952-3. Later I was disappointed when he did not
succeed John Charles. He would have been an excellent archbishop.

In any case Joe Carroll arrived for confirmation in good time
and was pleasant, urbane, good-humoured but also as dignified
as usual. At that time Hugh was responsible in theory for the
altar-boys, though in practice this role was filled by Hilda
Muston. As a teenager she had learned to serve Mass and for
over 60 years presided with remarkable tact over the sacristy
and the altar-boys, whom she treated like an extended family.
Five minutes before the confirmation ceremony was to begin she
called Rex aside, told him that there were no altar-boys and that
she had reminded Hugh to prepare the six best of them for the
ceremony.

Unfortunately Hugh was held up on his way to the church
and arrived some minutes after the time the ceremony was to
begin. He was met by Hilda outside the sacristy who alerted him
to the situation. He went into the altar-boys' sacristy to see for
himself! Then he came into the priests' sacristy and with his
large, infectious smile and extended hands announced: 'No
altar-boys! It could happen to a bishop.' Poor Tom Barry was
very embarrassed. Rex was furious and looking at me through
his clenched teeth whispered: 'Imbecile'! My chief concern was
that Joe Carroll would assume that I was responsible for the
mix-up, as at that time the junior curate was usually responsible
for the altar-boys. By that time it was also clear that Joe Carroll,
generally a model of equanimity, was not seeing any humour in
the situation.

Hugh who was to act as master of ceremonies got down to
work. He handed the bishop's mitre to Rex who refused to take
it. Then he attempted to give me the crozier but to my discredit I
kept my hands in my pockets. The result was that Hugh led out

the procession like a householder returning home with the weekly shopping – he had the mitre, the crozier and the missal all clasped to his chest. He was kept very busy during the early part of the ceremony, coping with what three or four altar-boys would normally be doing. As the bishop sat at the sanctuary gate making the sign of the cross on each confirmand and Hugh, as was usually done by the altar-boy, knelt in front of him with the missal leaning on his forehead and tilted towards the bishop. Hugh was becoming bald at that time and looked most incongruous in that position. I looked over at Rex. He winked and I could just about control myself. Thereafter rather belatedly we came to Hugh's rescue.

Tom Barry did not have much time to enjoy the relief of having the new parish established at Kill O' the Grange and the debt on Monkstown parish reduced to £50,000. He made a few visits to hospital and then suddenly we learned he was fatally ill from cancer. This he had kept a closely-guarded secret. I was in to see him in hospital two days before he died and was very moved by his emotional expression of kind regards for me.

Fr Tom Murphy who succeeded Tom Barry came with a high reputation as a pastoral man and lived up to his diocesan rating. He fitted in well in the Monkstown scene and, as Rex would say, 'made no waves'. He was far more enthusiastic than Tom Barry in updating the liturgy in accordance with the reforms of Vatican II. In a short time with his friend, Andy Devane, the distinguished architect, he had completed a tasteful refurbishment of the sanctuary in St Patrick's.

Soon after Tom Murphy's arrival a large, ugly lump appeared on Rex's forehead. It was diagnosed as a malignant tumour in the brain. We were all devastated. He was subsequently in hospital and then spent several months recuperating. He spent the last part of his convalescence with the Columban Fathers at Dalgan Park, near Navan, and said he could never speak highly enough of their generosity and kindness to him.

When Rex returned to the parish he was strangely quiet but he was as attentive as ever to his basic duties. His condition,

however, was never far from his mind. On one occasion he remarked to me how persons who came to see a priest very often
began the interview by saying: 'I have a problem, Father.' He
said that at that time he was often tempted to reply: 'Haven't we
all?'

The beginning of the end came for Rex during a Holyday
Mass on 8th December, feast of the Immaculate Conception. He
became totally confused and we had to lead him off the altar. He
spent a week in Monkstown hospital, where the staff could not
have been more kind to him. Then he flew home to Cork to his
sister Mary, Mrs Johnny Cahalane, to whom he always had been
very close. He died the following morning. His funeral Mass
was in the North Cathedral in Cork. It was attended by a large
number of his Dublin colleagues. The Cork priests were also
well represented, no doubt recalling the loss of Rex's brother, Fr
Eddie, in the crash of the Aer Lingus plane at Tuskar Rock, off
the Wexford coast, in March 1968. During the Mass I recalled
how much affection I had for Rex and, to my intense embarrassment, I wept.

When Rex became ill his extra duties were divided between
me and Val Carroll who had succeeded Hugh. This arrangement
continued between me and Fr Bertie Moore, who later succeeded
Val Carroll. One of the extra duties which I took up was the
chaplaincy of Monkstown Hospital. With generous support
from the Society of Friends this had been founded by Dr William
Plant in 1812 to serve the local community. But from the 1850s
onwards it was in effect a Protestant hospital for Protestant people. There was more than a whiff of bigotry about the place as
late as the 1960s. About the time Rex became chaplain and during his service there the ethos of the hospital was totally
changed. Rex gave most of the credit for this to the matron, Miss
Murphy, whom Rex referred to as 'an enlightened person'. In
this regard the secretary of the hospital board, who was a neighbour and close friend of Mgr Tom O'Donnell of Rathfarnham,
also had an important role, as had Rex himself. In the hospital I
followed the routine pioneered by Rex, visiting three times a

week, including a Communion round once a week and being available for emergency calls.

Bigotry was not something one associated with Canon Billy Wynne, the Church of Ireland rector, nor indeed with his successor, Reverend Kevin Dalton. We conducted most of our joint ecumenical services with Billy, and his flock and the other 'Separated Brethren' on neutral territory, generally in the chapel of the Sacred Heart Convent or in the refurbished Society of Friends Meeting House. Billy and Rex were close friends. Rex used to say of Billy that 'he fitted in'.

Rex liked to host a little supper, including a few drinks, for his clerical friends occasionally. Billy was always invited and generally came. I remember one most enjoyable session. For some reason Bishop Pat Dunne was present. He had probably been out to preside at some ecumenical or other service in the parish. Pat was delightful company and manifestly enjoyed soirees of that kind. He was like everybody's favourite uncle. In appearance he was corpulent and roly poly in shape with a handsome face. He had an appetite for food and a few drinks which belied his advanced age.

At this particular session Billy Wynne was immensely curious about the Vatican Council and quizzed Pat a great deal about it. Pat was enthralling on the subject. I must confess I was more taken by his many asides on the antics of the fathers of the council than on the theological insights he conveyed on the various important deliberations. Pat was an excellent raconteur. He recalled how moving it was to be one of the 3,000 or so cardinals, archbishops and bishops of the world filing in procession into St Peter's for the formal sessions. As he and the other council fathers stood in their places in St Peter's awaiting the entry of the Holy Father for the closing session, he said he found himself next to a very tall man who introduced himself as Robert Emmet Lucey, archbishop of San Antonio. Pat indicated his name and the fact that he was auxiliary bishop in Dublin. The tall man reflected on this and then asked Pat how long he was auxiliary bishop. Pat replied: 'Twenty years.' The archbishop reflected on this once more and then leaning confidentially towards Pat asked, 'What did you do?' Billy Wynne enjoyed this story even more than the rest of us.

For over fifty years Pat Dunne was the most influential and popular priest in the archdiocese. He was one of Archbishop William Walsh's secretaries from 1919 to 1921 and Archbishop Edward Byrne's chief secretary from 1921 to 1940. He helped John Charles to take over responsibility for the archdiocese in 1940 and acted as his vicar general from 1943 to 1946 and auxiliary bishop from 1946 to 1971. Thereafter he served as auxiliary bishop to Archbishop Dermot Ryan from 1971 to 1975. He was parish priest of the Holy Family parish, Aughrim Street, from 1943 to 1947 and of St Mary's parish, Haddington Road, from 1947 to 1988.

I am in no doubt that Pat Dunne was the chief foundation on which John Charles' remarkably successful archiepiscopacy was based. In 1940 the new archbishop was a Holy Ghost missionary priest – a rank outsider. Pat's exemplary loyalty to the new appointee ensured that of the senior clergy. This was not to say that Pat was not his own man. He always was. That was his great merit. An outstandingly able person, he was by nature modest and unassuming which made him all the more influential. Pat's popularity with generations of priests of the archdiocese was well deserved. A consummate peace-maker, he settled many serious personnel problems far from the gaze of John Charles.

The contrast between Pat and John Charles was striking. While John Charles looked the ascetic he was, it was obvious that Pat had a more easy-going life-style. John Charles was uncomfortable in almost any company, Pat enjoyed all company. The contrast between John Charles and Pat was well epitomised during their visits to parishes for the ceremony of confirmation. John Charles arrived and departed in the style of a foreign dignitary. Pat would suddenly be found to have arrived in the sacristy.

After the confirmation political correctness at that time did not require archbishops and bishops to go out front and in the

manner of politicians running for office shake the hand of everyone within reach and even kiss babies! Generally speaking John
Charles would leave almost immediately for another appointment. Pat would loiter around the sacristy in his shirt sleeves,
chatting with anyone within range. Later, as much as anyone
else, he would enjoy the festive meal provided by the parish
priest. An excellent, if cautious, conversationalist before leaving
for home he would have heard all the tittle tattle of the parish
and much of the current gossip of the archdiocese. The result
was that he had an encyclopaedic knowledge of the archdiocese
and especially its personnel. This he never failed to use to the
benefit of his co-diocesans from the oldest to the youngest.

In 1972 Dermot Ryan succeeded John Charles and continued
the development of the archdiocese apace. During this episcopacy
from 1972 to 1984, 62 parishes were constituted and formally
opened, different religious orders taking responsibility for
many of them. This development, matched by similar developments in the area of schools and social institutions of various
kinds necessitated a radical updating of the bureaucratic capacity
of archbishop's house. This was completed by Dermot Ryan and
in so doing he proved to be a most competent administrator and
an imaginative innovator. Dermot was known to have had more
than ordinary ambitions. So there was not undue surprise when
he was appointed prefect of the Congregation of the
Propagation of the Faith in the Vatican. Sadly he died in 1984
before he had an opportunity to show that he could repeat on
the world stage his remarkable achievements in Dublin. He left
the archdiocese a number of important legacies. Chief among these
was his establishment of the archdiocesan-wide Share collection.
This second collection at every public Mass on Sundays and
Holydays was set aside for the unprecedented growth then
taking place and it was to become a crucial factor in ensuring the
financial viability of the archdiocese. There was also his single-
minded insistence that the religious orders who had houses
within his jurisdiction would take responsibility for parishes
and in this way play their full part in the service of the people of
the archdiocese.

At this time I was elected to the 4th Dublin Diocesan Priests Council and served on it from 1975 to 1978. I found the experience frustrating. The Catholic Church never has been, is not and never will be a democracy. This pertains to the nature of the church as an institution and is something which I have never had difficulty in accepting. A body such as the Diocesan Priests Council tends to raise the unreal expectation that through it archdiocesan policy and practice can be determined. This is far from the case and it is only when this is appreciated that a body such as the Priests Council can become a useful vehicle for consultation.

In the early 1970s the conflict in Northern Ireland grew steadily worse. In August 1971 the British government introduced internment and 342 persons were interned without trial. As a result there was widespread communal violence during which 17 persons died and with the collusion of elements of the security forces 150 Catholic/Nationalist/Republican families had their houses burned. Hundreds of refugees streamed south out of Belfast and some were accommodated in an army camp opened for them in the Republic. Like many other people I was outraged by these developments.

In a sermon during the Masses on the following Sunday I was intensely critical of Britain's handling of the Northern Ireland crisis, in general, and these tragic developments in particular. I did not enjoy doing so, as quite a few of our most esteemed parishioners were persons who had served in various branches of the British armed services. In conclusion, apart from praying for peace and reconciliation, I acknowledged our powerlessness to do anything about the situation.

After one of the Masses Mark Hyland, a Fianna Fáil member of Dún Laoghaire Corporation, informed me that he and a few friends had set up a committee to collect funds to help the dependants, that is, the wives and children, of the internees. He was chairman of the committee with Dr Liam Connolly as secretary. Mark and Liam Connolly invited me to become president of the committee. I requested a week to consider the invitation. During that time I established that the bulk of the funds to be collected were to be channelled to the Belfast St Vincent de Paul conferences attached to the parish of St Patrick's in Donegall Street and to the Holy Cross monastery in Ardoyne. Hilary Hopkins, a well-known member of the Society, was to liaise between the committee and those conferences. I also learned that Fr Seán Cahill, whom I knew as a student in St Patrick's College, Maynooth, was to be the channel through which funds would be distributed to St Vincent de Paul conferences elsewhere.

I served as president until the committee was wound up not long after the ending of internment. We wrote letters to the newspapers appealing for donations and for support for our fund-raising activities. Most of our funds were raised by organising countrywide raffles. However, there were other functions at which wood carvings and other items produced by the internees were auctioned. Neil Blaney, TD, his friend, Dessie Hynes, proprietor of 'O'Donoghues', Merrion Row, David Andrews, TD, Niall Andrews, TD, and Joe Cahill attended one or two of these functions. Their presence made me feel uncomfortable, as I felt it tended to unduly politicise the committee and its work. I continued to be an active member of the committee, as at that time there was no other vehicle for helping the dependants.

In the summer of 1975 a group consisting of members of the Redemptorist community in Clonard and some Protestant clergymen from the Shankhill Road proposed that youngsters from the Falls Road and Shankhill Road areas should spend a holiday together in the Republic. The group had the support of the British Red Cross/Northern Ireland and the suggestion was that these eleven to twelve year olds would pair off one from each side of the religious divide and be cared for by a family for a week. I received a letter seeking my support for the project. Seeing the merit of enabling these youngsters to mingle and lay the foundation of genuine friendship I enthusiastically promoted the project. Quite a few families in the parish took and entertained a couple of these youngsters for a week. We collected them at Lansdowne Road where we returned them at the end of the week.

In promoting the project I announced that I would be caring for two of the youngsters and that I would ask that they both be from the Shankhill. I did this to give a lead in not being partisan and to indicate my wish that we should all be particularly generous to the Shankhill contingent. Dr Michael O'Connor, a much valued friend, came to me and told me that this could jeopardise the whole project. A man wise in the ways of the world, Michael had retired from the British Army Medical Corps and had been a prisoner of the Japanese during World War II. He explained to me that, notwithstanding my best intentions, my action would be construed as an attempt to proselytise the youngsters. In the event, I cared for two youngsters from the Falls Road and my next door neighbours, Mick and Rita Hanney, cared for two visitors from the Shankhill. Mick, a fireman on flexy time with Dún Laoghaire fire-brigade, and I took time in taking the four from Belfast on outings. After the first few days the four spent most of the time in each other's company. The kids were very well behaved, although I was a little disconcerted on one occasion when overhearing one of my charges boasting that his teenage brother was 'a bomb expert' with some IRA company in Belfast!

Dr Tiede Herrema, a Dutch businessman, was abducted by members of the IRA in October 1975. It seems the motive for this crime was to force the release of some prisoners. The homes of Republican sympathisers all over the country were searched. I had a visit from four armed members of the Garda Special Branch who said they intended to search the presbytery. I objected and asked what they were looking for. I was merely advised by the Garda in charge to contact the minister for justice. To be fair as they went through the house a few of the Gardaí were as embarrassed as I was angry. When they began to rifle through my papers I said I was about to ring a solicitor and they left.

Subsequently I speculated that a number of factors had led to their 'visit'. There was my association with the Committee for the Dependants of the Internees. A year earlier a young IRA activist, who shared a surname with me, Michael Gaughan, had died on hunger-strike in Parkhurst Prison in the Isle of Wight. But, probably most of all, at the request of Dan Nolan of Anvil Books and the Stack family in Tralee I was preparing a biography of Austin Stack, which was eventually published early in 1977. In this regard by an unfortunate coincidence I was then meeting and conducting interviews with numerous IRA activists of a previous generation. Indeed, during the previous year I had been similarly engaged when preparing *Memoirs of Constable Jeremiah Mee, RIC* for publication.

Afterwards I made no fuss about the incident, realising that the Garda were simply doing their duty. But it was a disconcerting experience and I had a new appreciation of how fortunate I was to be residing in a democratic state where, when necessary, the police can be called to account. However, I cannot say that in the fevered atmosphere of the time were I residing in Northern Ireland and were the RUC or British army involved I would have taken the same calm and mature view of the raid.

It has often been said that the quality of life in a community is best measured by the extent to which it fosters and values its eccentrics. On this reckoning Monkstown was a most mature and sophisticated community. There were more eccentrics in Monkstown than there were in all the other parishes I had served in combined. Nobody was a keener observer or enjoyed their antics more than Mrs Peggy Guinness. An outstanding personality, Peggy was the widow of Ralph, former proprietor of 'The Punch Bowl' at the bottom of Booterstown Avenue. She was a native of Cork, where two of her uncles had been parish priests, and she had many priest friends.

Peggy always appeared as if on her way to an evening at the opera: fashionable clothes, dripping with jewellery, her perfume was detectable at five paces. She was very influential and popular throughout the parish. Highly intelligent, charming and with a marvellous sense of humour, she was embarrassingly kind and helpful to all the priests, including myself. She was active in the planned-giving, a member of the Meals on Wheels committee, where she was invaluable in ensuring that all 'the notables' in the parish took part in that project, and was always ready to help the priests in any way required.

Peggy greatly enjoyed organising the parish's annual sale of work. This she did each year not with a committee but with 'helpers'. She held the sale in the Knox Hall, generously loaned to us by Canon Billy Wynne. Peggy enjoyed not only the success of the sale of work but the little skirmishes that accompanied its preparation. Smilingly, she said to me on a number of occasions: 'Fr Tony. There is nothing like a sale of work to bring the very worst out in people.'

Peggy loved to regale her friends with amusing stories about the eccentrics in the parish. Apart from being a sharp observer she had an uncanny knack of being present whenever anything unusual occurred. I recall a fairly typical happening in the local chemist shop after the 10 o'clock Mass. Peggy was present, as were two of the 'grande dames' of the parish. A heated exchange broke out between them which I ignored. One of the ladies, in her early life, had been an Abbey actress, which fact she felt constrained to advertise constantly. On being worsted in the exchanges, she swooned! I rushed to get her a chair to sit on. As I was then getting her a glass of water, Peggy sidled up beside me and in a stage-whisper said: 'Fr Tony. Don't be too worried. That lady has always been a better actress off the stage than she was ever on it.'

Peggy and her sister, Kitty, were particularly generous to their friend, Eoin O'Mahony, who frequently availed of their hospitality and generally arrived unannounced and without even an overnight bag. A barrister and a native of Cork, he had tried his hand at a number of avocations, even standing as an independent candidate for the presidency. Eventually he became a genealogist and a broadcaster. His speciality was the landed gentry of Ireland in general, and their family skeletons in particular. He was generally known and enjoyed being so known as the Pope O'Mahony. He acquired this sobriquet when, on being asked as a child what he intended to be, he invariably replied: 'The Pope.' A delightful and childlike person, he was incapable of dishonesty or malice of any kind. I was always invited to call and meet Eoin, whenever he stayed with Peggy and Kitty. He was wonderful company, although his conversation tended to be something of a monologue. Eoin remained a bachelor throughout his life. This did not deter him from strongly advising his unmarried friends to marry. Time and time again he would say to them: 'You know, you must get married and make some girl happy and give pleasure to your friends.'

Eoin was a never-ending source of stories about the great and the good from almost every century. He was mainly concerned with their human frailties, but he never dismissed someone without mentioning one of their redeeming qualities. I recall his gloss on Rodrigo Borgia/Pope Alexander VI, generally regarded as the most unworthy successor to St Peter. Eoin said: 'Alexander VI was Spanish and the Italians, especially the Romans, hated him. They spread stories about him. He wasn't guilty of half the crimes they accused him of. He was a big man. A nasty dispute had broken out between Spain and Portugal in South America. They agreed that he should adjudicate on the matter. He called for a globe and drew a diagonal line down through the continent, dividing it between Spain and Portugal. He was a big man.'

While I spent some of the happiest years of my life in Monkstown, for me the parish also had very sad associations. Apart from the deaths of Tom Barry and Rex Hegarty, I lost my treasured housekeeper, Binnie Moran. When appointed to the curacy in East Wall in 1965, I advertised for a housekeeper. She was the first to call to see me. I invited her to stay for a month and see if it suited her. She did and was subsequently indispensable to me in East Wall and during my appointments in Drimnagh and Monkstown. A most competent person, with a strong personality, she was one of the most altruistic persons I ever met.

For me the circumstances of her death were particularly tragic. In November 1975 Anvil Books published my *Memoirs of Constable Jeremiah Mee, RIC*. At the suggestion of Dan Nolan,

proprietor of Anvil Books, I went home to Listowel to promote
it. Binnie came with me. I proposed in the one day I had at home
to do a round trip: Listowel, Tralee, Killarney, Cork, Mallow,
Listowel: visiting all the bookshops on the route. As I was collecting material for a biography of Austin Stack, I also had
arranged to conduct interviews with Dan Lucey, deputy editor
of the *Cork Examiner*, and Connie Neenan, then retired from the
Waterford Glass Company. Both had been IRA activists and had
been on the anti-treaty side in the civil war.

Ironically my mother and aunt suggested to Binnie that she
should accompany me to ensure that I would drive carefully.
After a long day: celebrating an early Mass in the local convent,
successful visits to the various bookshops in the different towns
and two very useful interviews: I headed out of Cork on a dark
November evening. As was my practice I took two short-cuts
across the mountainous area on the Cork-Kerry-Limerick bor-
der. The first enabled me to by-pass Rock Chapel, the second
Abbeyfeale. On the first short route as I drove across Taur
mountain I ran into thick fog, the negotiation of which left me
exhausted. Then as I headed for home, again over high ground, I
feel asleep at the wheel and crashed into the projecting parapet
wall of a narrow bridge.

The crash left me unconscious until just before I was extricated
from the car and lifted into an ambulance from the county hospital in Tralee. Binnie, it seems, never lost consciousness but
suffered a broken femur. I was more fortunate. Apart from a
head wound, loss of blood and being badly shaken all over, I
had no serious injury. The car was a total write off. After ten
days I was allowed to return, much shaken, to Monkstown.
Binnie appeared to be also making good progress and I was
arranging to have her transferred to Dublin. A few days later I
received a phone call one morning at 4 am from Fr Bill Radley.
He told me he had given Binnie the Last Rites and that shortly
afterwards she had died, owing, it seems, to blood clotting.

I was devastated by the news. Binnie was buried in the family
grave at Glenmore in County Kilkenny. It was with great difficulty and only with the assistance of Binnie's nephew, Fr Don

Moran, that I managed to conclude her concelebrated funeral Mass. It took me over a year to get over the sorrow and deep regret I felt at her death and particularly the circumstances of it.

Not long after Binnie had died Gretta O'Brien called on me. This turned out to be one of the most fortunate events which ever happened to me. She said she had heard that I was on the look-out for a housekeeper. While my mind was not yet focused in that direction, I invited her to stay for a month and see if she liked Monkstown. She had previously been a priest's house-keeper in the parishes of Cabra West, Crumlin, Dolphin's Barn, Larkhill and Narraghmore. I find it well-night impossible to adequately express my indebtedness to her for her kindness, loyalty and support since that first meeting.

Early in 1977 Fr Vinnie Quilter, classmate and life-long friend, phoned me enquiring what the curacy in Monkstown was like. I told him it was idyllic and that I hoped to be left there for a few more years. Vinnie, with good reason, was the most popular member of our class. He was very successful and well-liked in all his appointments. However, from his forties onwards he did not enjoy good health. At that time he was a curate in Roundwood in County Wicklow.

It seems that on medical grounds it was decided that he should be transferred to some curacy, with more easy access to a hospital. He had discussed this with the authorities and had opted for Monkstown! Like all of us Vinnie had his failings. One of his was that he found it difficult to keep anything confidential. On the occasion he rang me, after a characteristically long, chatty and even garrulous conversation, he blurted out that he would be replacing me in the summer changes.

I was not at all impressed and told him so. However, I kept the information confidential and made no fuss. But I was not looking forward to the summer changes. I knew I would be on the move but I did not know where I would end up.

CHAPTER 10

St Thérèse's, Mount Merrion
1977-1983

In the summer of 1977 I was appointed to a curacy in the parish of St Thérèse, Mount Merrion, replacing Fr Dinny Bergin who had been placed in charge of the parish of the Virgin Mary at Ballymun. I already had happy associations with Mount Merrion. Tim O'Brien, first cousin and life-long friend of my mother, resided at The Rise near the presbytery. My mother was very proud of her cousin Tim, secretary of the department of lands, telling me frequently that he was the youngest civil servant ever appointed to head a government department.

Over many years I was indebted to him and his wife, Kay, for many kindnesses. When sitting for my BA in mid-September 1953 I was a guest of the O'Brien's who did everything to ensure I was successful in my examination. Tim and Kay were at my ordination and the subsequent reception. I celebrated my first Mass in Dublin for the family in the Church of St Thérèse, with their two sons, Brian and Aidan, then altar-boys, assisting. Subsequently I had an open invitation to call to O'Briens at any time, an invitation I liberally availed of. For about 20 years I spent St Patrick's Day with the family attending with Tim and Kay, until the fixture was dropped, the Railway Cup inter-provincial finals in Croke Park. Also over the years Tim and I attended many of the Kerry team's matches in Croke Park. By a curious irony I spent less time in O'Briens' when I resided across the road from them than when I was in any other parish.

When I was in Mount Merrion Tim's brother, Patrick, had come to reside with them. Patrick had retired after a life-time of service in the Royal Navy. After graduating in medicine at TCD he entered the naval service. A handsome, distinguished-looking and charming man, he had a fund of stories about his service on the 'China station', that is, in a naval squadron off Hong Kong, his experience of having the destroyer on which he was serving sunk in a battle in the Mediterranean in World War II and the idyllic time he spent as medical officer on the Royal Yacht *Britannia* during Queen Elizabeth's II's first triumphant visit to Australia. After his death I was delighted when a well-deserved laudatory obituary which I had written on him was published in the *Irish Times* and a TCD *alumni* publication.

The parish of Mount Merrion-Kilmacud was constituted from Dundrum in 1948 and Mount Merrion and Kilmacud were separated into two parishes in 1964. To Mgr Joe Deery must go the bulk of the credit for building up the parish of Mount Merrion and having its beautiful church completed. When I arrived in the parish it consisted of some 2,000 families. It was compact and was entirely middle-class and upper middle-class.

Canon Ardle MacMahon was the parish priest and my fellow-curates were Frs Con McGillycuddy and Pat Sheehan. Ardle McMahon prior to his appointment had spent his life as a priest, apart from some years engaged in post-graduate studies in Rome, as secretary to Archbishops McQuaid and Ryan. Exemplary in his dedication to his priestly duties, he manifestly enjoyed being at the service of his parishioners. Con McGillycuddy was a priest with considerable pastoral experience and a fellow Kerryman. Pat Sheehan was a member of the Missionaries of the Sacred Heart order and, after helping with various projects at the Catholic Communications Centre, had been co-opted into the parish. Con was succeeded by Dermot Lane who in turn gave way to Alan Mooney, each of whom served for short periods in the parish.

One of the features of the parish as far as I was concerned was the fine residence I moved into as my new presbytery. At the corner of the church car park it had been the show-house when the builders were selling the houses on The Rise, and Dinny Bergin had just had it renovated before I arrived.

It had a lovely garden front and back which Tom Doyle came

each Wednesday to tend. He was a native of Shillelagh, County Wicklow, and in his youth worked on the Coolattin estate. At the outbreak of World War II he was persuaded by the estate manager, a retired major, to enlist in the British army and served in Field Marshal Bernard Montgomery's 8th army. The war took him through North Africa, Sicily, Italy and into Germany. When the war ended he was a bat-man to a high-ranking officer in London for a year before being demobbed. He had lunch with me every Wednesday and, though very modest and unassuming, enthralled us with his experiences. These had left him a most devout and prayerful Catholic. When Tom, a bachelor, became too old to work I managed to get suitable accommodation for him with the Little Sisters of the Poor at Roebuck. He was very happy there, largely because he was within a short distance of the chapel, where he spent a lot of time each day praying in front of the Blessed Sacrament. Later I felt very privileged in being able to celebrate his requiem Mass.

In Mount Merrion there were the usual priestly duties: Masses, confessions, preaching, duty-days and 1st Friday calls to the house-bound, as well as attending to 'the rites of passage': baptisms, marriages and funerals. With regard to Masses we provided the people with a superb service. On each weekday there were Masses at 7.30, 8, 10 and 7.30 p.m. and on the weekend a vigil Mass and seven Masses on Sunday. Each priest had two sessions of confessions every Saturday. Ardle MacMahon's confessional was somewhat unusual. A keen linguist, he was fairly proficient in French, German, Italian and Spanish. Signs indicating this bedecked his confessional. This led, I must confess, to his colleagues always referring to his confessional as the language school!

First Friday and urgent calls tended to be light. This was the direct result of affluence. As soon as the elderly became ill or difficult to cope with they were generally transferred into a hospital or a nursing-home.

There was one urgent call I shall never forget. A housewife in her mid-forties decided to commit suicide. She poured a gallon of petrol over herself and set herself alight. It was summer time and a neighbour in the next garden saw her and rang me. I told her to ring Dr Margaret Daly immediately. By the time I arrived the unfortunate woman was black all over and burnt like a cinder. Incredibly she was still alive and shrieking with pain. As I knelt beside her, she managed to recite the act of contrition with me. I gave her absolution and then she continued to recite 'Hail Marys' with me. Within minutes, thankfully, Dr Daly arrived and gave her an injection of morphine in the ankle, the only place available for this, and put her out of her pain. Dr Daly's arrival on the scene so quickly was typical. She was a most caring, committed and popular GP and, incidentally, the sister of Fr Jimmy Alston, then a curate in Booterstown. For me the most unforgettable aspect of this tragic incident was the appalling smell of burning human flesh.

Like my fellow-curates I had responsibility for a district which included about 700 houses. As was my practice I had a visiting card printed and called on each of them once a year. My district included the upper middle class end of the parish, mainly, the Palms and Ardilea estates. The latter was a particularly salubrious locality with the various roads named after famous universities. On visiting these estates I discovered the profile of the very prosperous at that time: senior executives in drug companies (legal ones, of course!), the chief representatives of the major oil companies, property owners, proprietors of factories and businesses, senior members of the legal and medical professions and some senior academics from nearby UCD.

One of my tasks was to act as chaplain to Oatlands Christian Brothers Primary School. It was established in 1954 and at this time had 320 pupils and an excellent principal, the youthful Brother James Kelly. I taught a class period in Religious Knowledge to a different class each week. The new catechetical programme had been introduced. Unprompted by me most of the lay-teachers, all of whom had about 20 years teaching experience, expressed misgivings about the new programme. Almost from the outset I was less than convinced that it was an improvement on what it replaced. This programme, it seemed to me, owed more to the fashionable excessively child-centred trends in education at this time than to any directives from Vatican II. In due course one effect which was becoming more and more obvious to me was that in every school the youngsters had much less knowledge and especially far less accurate knowledge about their faith.

Another of my duties was to act as chaplain to the Girl Guides and their juniors: the *Brigíní*. They shared a premises/ den with the Boy Scouts, whose chaplain was Con McGillycuddy. The Boy Scouts had independently of the parish built the den and both troops flourished. I dropped in each week to the Girl Guides and *Brigíní*. The two leaders were very dedicated and enthusiastic and were assisted by a number of parents. The *Brigíní* always appeared to me to be like little furry rabbits. More frequently than I wished, I was inveigled into joining in their little games.

When I arrived in Mount Merrion ecumenism was flourishing in the parish. The first clerical visitor who came to my presbytery to welcome me into the parish was Reverend Desmond Black, minister in charge of the local Presbyterian church. The happy state of ecumenism was due in no small measure to Ardle and to Fr Pat Devine who was very active in this regard when in the parish. This is probably the reason why almost ever since then the latter has been the diocesan secretary for ecumenism. I, jointly with Desmond Black, had responsibility for a committee which dealt with the social events encouraging ecumenism. Tom Murray, chairman of the ESB and father of Bishop Donal, was the chairman. Tom was a person from whom one learned a great deal. Mrs Maura Kilcullen, mother of Justin, director of Trócaire, was the other representative of the RCs. There were two representatives each from the Church of Ireland and the Presbyterian community.

The committee organised an annual golf outing from the three parishes and an Ecumenical Ball. Much of the work organising the Ball was done by the Church of Ireland representative,

Harry Booker and his charming wife Rhona, who were close friends of Canon Trevor Hipwell. This Ecumenical Ball, held each year at the Killiney Castle Hotel, was well-attended and most enjoyable. Harry was a member of the headquarters staff of the IRFU and one offshoot of my friendship with him was my obtaining complimentary tickets for home rugby internationals. Generally the seat at the matches would be so central that, were I to stretch out my arm, I could almost touch one of the reserves of the visiting team.

I had other commitments in the parish. Each first Friday of the month I had confessions for the girls of the Sacred Heart Convent Secondary School at Mount Anville and afterwards Mass for them at noon in their school chapel. I took turns with the other curates to provide weekly confessions for the patients, mostly the elderly poor, in Linden Convalescent Home and Talbot Lodge, both run by the Irish Sisters of Charity. In 1971 the Irish Sisters of Charity gave part of their Linden property for use as Madonna House, where foundlings and children, in need of care from five days to five years, were cared for. In 1977 Sister Carmel, tireless champion of such children, who was in charge of the project from the outset, set up a 'village' where 'families' of 10 to 12 children were accommodated. At her request, I provided Mass for her, the staff and the older children at noon every Wednesday.

The residents of Mount Merrion seemed to have everything, at least in material terms. But, it seemed to me, many of them were strangely lacking in a sense of community. I was given some anecdotal evidence of this. Some of them did not seem to know even the names of people who resided near them in the same road for some twenty years. Then a number of young mothers contacted me and asked me to organise baby-sitting so that they could get out of the house more. I met a group of them and indicated that what I had in mind and intended to set up was a kind of co-operative of baby-sitters, whereby they could facilitate each other. They very quickly told me that none of them was willing to baby-sit other people's children and that what they wanted was that I should arrange that a number of school-girls be organised who would provide the service and be paid for it. Up to then I had not met that kind of attitude expressed so directly. A few years earlier Ardle had proposed that a 'Neighbours Group' set about promoting a better sense of community in the parish. To this end and to get people, especially the younger women, to know each other, to mingle and be prepared to help each other I decided to organise a coffee morning in our community hall open to all every Thursday. Mrs Catherine Doyle and Mrs Rosemary Sheehan, two 'medical' wives and excellent young women, helped me with this and ensured its success.

One of the tasks which I regarded as a chore was attending the monthly meeting of the parish council. This had been established by Ardle, was elected in some way, consisted of about 50 members and had a usual attendance of about 30. The meeting was on the third Thursday of each month at 8 pm. It could last 2 to 3 hours. At Ardle's request I always attended. He was such a decent, dedicated and sincere person I just could not refuse and anyway I have never been very good at inventing excuses.

The meetings would drone on about almost every trivial matter in the parish. Then occasionally something substantive would arise and Ardle would have to tell the meeting, in effect, that the decision on it would be made not by the meeting but by him. When this occurred the embarrassment all round would be almost palpable. Many of the members of the parish council were highly talented, senior civil servants or other such people. I always suspected they attended for the same reason as I did, namely, their high regard for Ardle.

On a few occasions I discussed the merits or otherwise of the parish council with Ardle, I recall rather provocatively asking him how many similar-type parish councils there were in the archdiocese at that time. He replied there were two: his and one established by Canon John Kelly. It was significant, I pointed out, that neither he nor John Kelly, who had spent his entire life in Clonliffe, ever had any pastoral experience before being appointed parish priests. Also I suggested that it was strange, if parish councils were so useful, that none of the other 160 or 170 parish priests in the archdiocese had established them.

Since that time I have noted that those who in the various pastoral journals champion elected parish councils almost without exception never had the responsibility of running a parish. And the few of them that did generally tended to resign that responsibility rather quickly. My opinion on parish councils is that where they are considered to be useful, as they sometimes are, they should be small and representative of different areas of the parish but never elected. They should be advisory and clearly described as such and ought to be handled with great sensitivity, as they can very easily become divisive and centres of factionalism owing to the activities of single-agenda driven members.

Preaching was particularly important in Mount Merrion, as the congregations were generally 'switched on'. Each of us preached in our turn at the eight Masses each weekend. We were fortunate to be joined in the rota by Fr Dominic Johnson, a Benedictine. At that time he was in charge of a student hostel in Rathgar for past pupils of Glenstal Abbey School who were attending university. He was a friend of Ardle's and told him he would like to do some parish/pastoral work. Ardle was delighted to facilitate him and Dominic celebrated the 11 o'clock Mass every Sunday and preached in his turn. An excellent preacher, he gave one of the best sermons I ever heard, crafting it along the lines of an Eamonn Andrews 'This is Your Life' programme.

Dominic invariably began his homily by referring to a main news item during the previous week. He did this to ensure the congregation's attention. I always considered this superfluous, as in my experience any congregation who sits up for a sermon will give a preacher a minute's attention straight away. It is after that he has to work to keep them focused. In my case at that time an intractable strike had been continuing intermittently at Blackrock Post Office. Dominic referred to this and the fact that the government, then a Fianna Fáil administration, were not very successful in dealing with it. Dominic was by nature and nurture a Fine Gael voter and at the 11 o'clock Mass, realising that he might be sounding rather partisan, added that the strike had begun and had not been successfully been dealt with under the previous Fine Gael/Labour government.

What followed was like something out of a Gilbert and Sullivan light opera. When Dominic was leaving the sacristy after Mass he was accosted by members of the local Fine Gael Cumann and accused of slighting the party and the previous government. But that was not all. Garret FitzGerald, the Fine Gael leader, resided locally. While Ardle was having his lunch a two-page letter of complaint about Dominic from Garret was delivered by hand. It seems Dominic's remark posed a serious danger to the foundations of parliamentary democracy and the trust of Irish people in politics and politicians. In the context of what Dominic actually said it was ironic that Garret warned him against unfairly promoting the interests of any party in government at the expense of any other. I had scarcely finished my lunch when Ardle was at my door with this letter. At that time he had developed a habit of consulting me about practically everything. On reading the letter I offered Ardle three options: (1) to ignore the letter, thereby indicating he did not receive letters which were a nonsense, (2) sending a simple polite acknowledgement immediately or (3) delaying that acknowledgement for about a week. He opted for (3), although I told him my preference would have been (1).

I suggested to Ardle that he not mention the complaint to Dominic, as he might have been unduly upset by it. Dominic was under a bit of pressure at that time. He liked to engage in public discourse through the columns of the *Irish Times*. His letters invariably had a centre-right political flavour. About that time the Irish Rugby Union was resisting pressure to join a sports' boycott of South Africa. The Irish apartheid movement responded by organising extensive picketing of high-profile rugby matches. Dominic upheld the right of people to attend matches and not to be prevented from doing so by those protesting about apartheid or any other issue. He especially deprecated the manner in which politics and sport were being linked. The clear consensus among the rest of us on the Mount Merrion staff was that human rights were far more important than politics and sport combined. Because Dominic was such a gentlemanly and pleasant person – he had a lot in common with the legendary James Dillon – none of us confronted him on his view on the issue, although he could have been in no doubt as to ours.

The incident involving Dominic Johnson was not the last experience I had of how thin-skinned some politicians can be. In June 1979 Garret FitzGerald formally opened a new centre for the St John of God Brothers near the roundabout at Sallynoggin. It was to provide residential services for children and adults with varying degrees of learning disability. Garret was reported in the press as praising the Brothers for their wonderful work. Then he strayed from his immediate topic to deprecate the fact that priests who had authority in the church were elderly and celibate and so presumably not quite up to carrying out their responsibilities adequately. He was also reported as having criticised the undue emphasis in sermons on sexual morality, while neglecting the imperatives of justice, including the obligation to pay income tax. At the time Edward Heath, bachelor and not a young man, was prime minister in the UK. I also recalled the service such 'geriatrics' as Konrad Adenauer and Charles de Gaulle had given to their respective nations. I knew from listening for some thirty years to the sermons of my colleagues that his assumption about sex being referred to frequently therein was nonsense. I drafted the following and it was published at the bottom of the letters page in the *Irish Times* of 22 June 1979:

Sir,

I noted with interest Dr Garret FitzGerald's suggestion that priests should preach more sermons on the moral obligation to pay income tax and on the inherent evil in the evasion thereof. May I suggest to those who intend to oblige Dr FitzGerald that one of the first points worth considering on this topic is the fact that of all the sections in the community Dr FitzGerald and his colleagues in the Oireachtas *alone*

enjoy a large part of their income tax free. The injustice and
anti-democratic character of this is compounded by the fact
that they actually make this law to suit themselves.

J. Anthony Gaughan, CC,
79 The Rise,
Mount Merrion,
Co Dublin.

I had a reply from Garret not in the columns of the *Irish Times*
but in a four page letter addressed to me personally. The drift of
it did not go far beyond the theme that comments such as mine
could shake the foundations of our tender democracy, mainly
by causing the Irish people to lose trust in politicians. He also set
out to demonstrate that any advantage TDs enjoyed *vis-à-vis* the
rest of us with regard to the payment of income tax was not
something for which they were responsible! I enjoyed replying
to his various statements, especially this last ludicrous claim.

At the time a neighbour friend of mine in the parish had just
retired from the Office of the Revenue Commissioners. A highly
placed executive he was almost disbelieving when I told him of
the content of the letter I had received. He volunteered to let me
have as much embarrassing information as I wished to obtain on
the salaries and especially the expenses claimed by TDs. I told
him I was not interested in pursuing the matter and I replied
similarly to the editor of one of the Catholic weeklies who asked
me to write a few articles on the subject.

In the meantime I received a reply from Garret to my letter.
This second letter merely showed that he could condense to two
pages what he had extended to four pages in his first letter. I
acknowledged his letter and told him I was far too busy and had
not the secretarial assistance to engage in any further correspondence on the matter.

I also had a letter from John Horgan. I suppose, being the
Labour TD for the constituency in which Mount Merrion was
situated, he felt impelled to do so. I was again surprised when,
far from replying in the columns of the *Irish Times*, to which in
the past he had given signal service, he too wrote me a personal

letter. Thankfully he did not attempt to demonstrate that Dáil Éireann was not ultimately responsible for the salaries and other emoluments of TDs. However, he did adopt a rather novel approach. He set out to assure me that the Dublin Corporation workers who collected refuse, when wet-time and over-time payments were added to their wages, were paid more than TDs. I was very friendly with John at that time and frequently met him, as he had facilities in our community centre for his con- stituency clinic. I decided on a humorous reply and wrote to him: 'On the subject of wages and salaries you write like a shop- steward.' John did not see any humour in this and ended our friendship. At the time Garret and John, whenever featured in the media, were quite robust in their criticism of all and sundry, not least various features of the Catholic Church. I was truly amazed at the concern my little peck caused them.

I had many close friends in Mount Merrion, among them Ossie Dowling, his wife Fran and son Rupert. Theirs was a close- knit family rendered all the closer by the tragic loss of a beautiful, eighteen-year-old daughter to leukaemia. Ossie headed the diocesan press office from 1965 to 1978. A much experienced journalist, he kindly checked the page proofs of a few of my books.

In 1978 Ossie told me that *Time-Life* were publishing a series of coffee-table books for the international market on the great cities of the world, including Dublin. A photographer, named John McDermott, a third-generation Irish-American from California, was providing the pictures for it. He asked Ossie to help him obtain a picture of a typical Dublin priest. At Ossie's request I agreed to meet McDermott. In fact, I invited him to Sunday lunch.

Before lunch instead of relaxing and chatting with me, McDermott followed Gretta, my housekeeper, into her small kitchen. As she prepared the lunch, he snapped her about a dozen times from every conceivable angle. By that time she was not amused. When she served me my lunch, McDermott got up from the table and photographed the two of us. This is the picture he published and our mutual friends are convinced from our solemn expressions that we just had an almighty row! Ossie loved the picture. He said it was very natural! By a curious co-incidence the only other cleric to be featured in the *Time-Life* book *The Great Cities/Dublin* (1978) is George Henry. McDermott, it seems, snapped him at Glenmalure Park, as, bedecked in his Shamrock Rovers green and white scarf, he is cheering on his team. Sadly not long after my visit from John McDermott it became clear that Ossie was fatally ill from cancer. When he was dying in the Mater Hospital he sent for me and I stayed with him until he died.

Eamonn de Barra, who resided opposite me, was another close friend. A native of West Cork and as old as the century, he had been active in the Republican movement from 1916 on-wards. He served as IRA, OC, Intelligence for Great Britain, as late as 1927. A child-like person, incapable of ill-feeling towards anyone, he was one of the most idealistic persons I ever met. His two great passions were his religion and his country. Apart from Christ, his role model was Patrick Pearse. He was a life-long friend of Margaret, sister of the patriot, and with her ensured that St Enda's, Pearse's school, was preserved for the nation. He was also a leading member of the committee which rescued Kilmainham jail from falling into decay and having it made fit for storing and exhibiting mementoes of the struggle for indep-endence.

Eamonn was on first name terms with nearly all the major and many of the minor figures who were involved in the Anglo-Irish war. He was particularly insightful in describing the jock-eying between Michael Collins and his associates, on the one hand, and Eamonn de Valera and his supporters, on the other, in the period leading up to the civil war. An anti-treatyite, yet he had as fond recollections of his association with Michael Collins, as he had with Eamonn de Valera. Although he had retired from the Republican movement before the 1930s, Eamonn did not lose contact with his former comrades. In 1966, on the occasion of the 50th anniversary of the Easter Rising, he returned to Cork for the celebrations and had a wonderful time meeting old comrades. He was given an eye-witness account of the ambush which led to the tragic death of Michael Collins. This was agreed by the six people who were most closely involved in the incident. Subsequently he let me have this account and gave me permission to make use of it when all the participants named in it had died. Eventually I was able to make use of the account in my attempt in the *Irish Times* of 20 August 1988 to give a definitive description of the fateful ambush.

During my final year in Mount Merrion Eamonn developed a medical condition whereby the flow of blood to his brain was partially impeded. This led to his occasionally suddenly becoming unconscious and to some other bizarre behaviour. This strange behaviour consisted of his getting up in the middle of the night and rushing to a local shop for his daily newspaper. While Eamonn was over six feet and built accordingly, his wife, Eithne, sister of Mgr Feithín O'Doherty, was diminutive. She was also a very private person, was unwilling to call the emergency services or even her neighbours for help and invariably came for me to coax and / or frog-march Eamonn home and back into bed. After two or three months of this I was both relieved and thrilled when Eamonn's doctor discovered some drug or combination of drugs which almost entirely cured his condition and he had a further eight or nine years of relatively good health.

Con Murphy was another prominent parishioner in Mount Merrion. A native of North Cork, he had been in effect for many years personal assistant to Alfred O'Rahilly, president of UCC. Subsequently he was an executive in the Irish Sugar Company, where he acted in a similar capacity to the managing director, General Mickey Joe Costelloe. Eventually he was the first to be appointed to the position of rights commissioner in the Labour Court and he was particularly successful in settling numerous disputes which would otherwise have led to work stoppages through strikes.

A few years after Alfred O'Rahilly retired from UCC, he was

ordained. Thereafter he resided in the Castle, at Blackrock College. In the traumatic period covering the death of O'Rahilly's wife, his retirement from UCC and his preparation for the priesthood Con and his wife, Teresa, were particularly kind and helpful to him.

Throughout his life O'Rahilly had been collecting material with a view to publishing a comprehensive life of Jesus Christ. By the time he came to reside in the Castle some volumes had been published. He then set about preparing for publication a study of the passion and death of Christ. However, he died before it was completely ready for publication. O'Rahilly's close friends, Fr Michael McCarthy, CSSp, and Fr Michael O'Carroll, CSSp, made several unsuccessful attempts to have it finally edited and published. Through Con Murphy, a mutual friend, they appealed to me to take the work in hand. I did so. But it was nine years before I was finished with Alfred O'Rahilly, publishing not only his encyclopaedic *The Crucified* but a four-volume biography of that remarkable polymath.

In 1981 the parish celebrated the silver jubilee of the blessing and formal opening of the church of St Thérèse. To mark the occasion Archbishop Ryan conferred the *Bene Merenti* medal on Philomena McSweeney, principal of St Thérèse's national school, and on Jimmy Cruise, the sacristan, for their long and devoted service. All the priests who served in Mount Merrion were delighted that the ever-obliging Jimmy was honoured. By a curious coincidence Jimmy, who in his youth served in the army, remembered my uncle-in-law Captain Tom Shanahan, who for many years was in charge of recruits at the Curragh Camp. Also in connection with the silver jubilee, a new altar, constructed in accordance with the liturgical regulations of Vatican II, was dedicated by the archbishop. There were other celebrations, the highlight of which was a festive Mass concelebrated by the parochial clergy and the many priests serving in the archdiocese and elsewhere who were natives of the parish. At Ardle's request I prepared a booklet on the history of the area and the parish, *Mount Merrion, the old and the new* (1981). Fr Mick

Cleary at that time had his own radio programme and had launched a national appeal for aid to Ethiopia. We donated the profit from the booklet to Mick's Famine Fund.

In 1982 I had my own silver-jubilee – that of my ordination. During my life I have scarcely ever celebrated any birthday or any other personal anniversary. I intended that it should be no different on this occasion. However, Gretta, my housekeeper, decided otherwise. She had discovered in a drawer a photograph of the Dublin ordination class of 1957, which had been published in the *Irish Press*. She had it beautifully framed and presented it to me, along with an inscribed silver tray.

As we looked at the picture, she was curious as to the whereabouts of the 25 eager-looking, young priests. I proceeded to name each of them and where they were then ministering. However, three had sought to be laicised prior to getting married. This was something of which she strongly disapproved. When I came to the third of those classmates I felt a little joke might cover my embarrassment. So I said: 'I suppose I'll be off myself any day now when I head into my mid-life crisis.' Like a shot she replied: 'Don't be silly, Father. You are well beyond that!'

In 1998 the priests and people of Mount Merrion celebrated the jubilee of the institution of the parish. There was a concelebrated Mass on the feast of St Thérèse, titular saint of the parish. Archbishop Desmond Connell was the chief celebrant with about 40 concelebrants, including the staff, those who formerly served in the parish and natives of the parish. At the request of Ardle and the parish council, I was invited to preach the homily, an honour I greatly appreciated. I derived considerable satisfaction on being given an opportunity to outline the extraordinary contribution made to the educational and social well-being of the community by the Irish Sisters of Charity, the Sacred Heart Sisters and not least the Irish Christian Brothers.

CHAPTER 11

University Church, St Stephen's Green
1983-1988

In the summer of 1983 I was appointed to the curacy in the parish of Our Lady, Seat of Wisdom, better known as the parish of University Church on St Stephen's Green. I replaced Fr Frank McDonnell who had been transferred to the parish of Ballymore Eustace in County Kildare. University Church parish had been constituted from St Kevin's at Harrington Street in 1974.

University Church is the most visible of the legacies of John Henry Newman's time in Ireland. Born in London on 21 February 1801, Newman was educated at Oxford and he was ordained in the Anglican Church. From 1828 onwards he served as vicar of St Mary's, Oxford. While there he became the most prominent member of the Oxford Movement in England. The Movement called for a renewal of the Anglican Church as a more purely religious body. Members were known as the Tractarians from the *Tracts for the times* in which they presented their ideas. In his *Tract 90*, published in 1841, Newman made a systematic effort to reconcile the 39 Articles of statutory Anglican belief with Catholic doctrine. In the face of the bitter opposition of the Anglican authorities to his preaching and writing, he had to retire from St Mary's in 1843. He converted to Catholicism in 1845 and was ordained in 1847 in Rome, where he joined the Oratorians, an institute founded by St Philip Neri (1515-95).

On behalf of the Irish bishops Cardinal Paul Cullen invited Newman in 1851 to come to Dublin and establish a Catholic University. He accepted the invitation. From the outset he planned the erection of a university church which would be at the heart of the new institution, and would 'maintain and symbolise that great principle in which we glory as our characteristic, the union of science and religion'. The church was completed in 1856. While Newman's friend, John Hungerford Pollen, was the architect, painter and decorator of University Church, the plan and basic ideas with regard to its building and decoration were Newman's.

The Catholic University of Ireland (1854-1879), founded by Newman, evolved into University College (1879-1908) which was eventually absorbed into UCD, a constituent college of the National University of Ireland established in 1908. From 1964 onwards various faculties situated at Earlsfort Terrace were transferred to the new campus at Belfield. For over a hundred years Newman's church had continued to be the church of the university. Then in 1969 the Michael Devlin Memorial church was built at Belfield and thereafter served as the university church. But, although no longer the focus for the religious activities of undergraduates, Newman's church continues to be a popular venue for the marriages of graduates, religious services associated with class reunions and for special university occasions.

In the meantime from 1869 onwards University Church had also become a chapel of ease to St Kevin's parish in Harrington Street and from 1974 the church for the newly-constituted parish, hived off St Kevin's.

I was welcomed to University Church by Fr Fionán O'Sharkey, the second parish priest of this new parish. He had a brother who was a Carmelite priest and a sister in the Loreto order. His father was Dr Séamus Ó Searchaigh who lectured on Modern Irish in UCD and on Old Irish in St Patrick's College, Maynooth. He had a life-long interest in Newman, had celebrated his first Mass in University Church and was very attached to it. Ascetic in appearance and lifestyle, he paid great attention to his prayer-life. Each morning he spent about an hour at his *priedieu* before celebrating Mass. He was punctilious in attending to his priestly duties and was exceptionally generous to the poor.

The parish was very compact. It consisted of nearly all of the area circumscribed by Baggot Street, the Royal Canal, Harcourt

Street and St Stephen's Green. It included a night-club and red-light district. One learned very quickly not to stop the car after dark and ask a pedestrian for help to find an address! Apart from those in a few high-rise apartment blocks, very few people resided in the area.

Fionán and I each had a district. Neither of these had more than two hundred families. A significant number of the people in the area were elderly couples who resided in attic or basement flats. Their presence was considered useful by the proprietors of offices and businesses. I had a visiting card printed and each year called on the houses in my district. My home visitation, however, seldom went beyond leaving a visiting-card and up-dating the register left to me by Frank McDonnell.

University Church was a service church, most of its worshippers coming from outside the parish. We provided seven Masses each weekend: Vigil Mass at 7 pm and 8, 9, 10,11, 12 and 5.30 pm on Sunday. The week-day morning Masses were at 8 and 10. Confessions were very light, a half-hour at noon on Saturday. A member of the community at the Holy Ghost major seminary at Kimmage Manor came to celebrate the 11 and 12 o'clock Masses each Sunday.

I had only six 1st Friday calls. One was to Liam O'Flaherty, acclaimed writer and stormy petrel of the 1920s and 1930s. Although in good physical condition, his health had declined considerably in other areas. He had a magnificent mane of white hair and shouted as if he was in the open air, whenever he spoke. He was delighted on one occasion when I invited him to attend as my guest an annual dinner of Irish Pen, of which he had been a member years earlier. However, when I called for him his doctor was present and advised that the occasion would have been too stressful for him.

Jim and Mary Carey were also on my 1st Friday list. They resided in two rooms above a barber's shop in Lower Baggot Street. Jim had served on the Western front in World War I and subsequently had been a doorman in a Dublin hotel. There was a fragrance of goodness, holiness and happiness about them.

Their lives were imbued by their Faith. I found their respect for the priest a rather humbling experience. They had no family and for many years the great focus of their lives was the Perpetual Adoration of the Blessed Sacrament conducted in the chapel of the Sisters of Marie Reparatrice in nearby Lower Fitzwilliam Street.

Much of the priest's time at University Church was occupied with answering the telephone and interviewing couples who were to marry there. There were as many as 140 marriages each year. The requirement that the couples had to be graduates had long since been waived. Some of those marrying in the church would have a priest-relative or priest friend to conduct the ceremony but most would not. When Fionán was on holiday I had on a number of Saturdays to celebrate three Nuptial Masses and dash around and put in a short appearance at each of the receptions. When I arrived at University Church Fionán had set the fee for marriages for 'outsiders' at £30. I persuaded him to raise it to a £100. We then prepared an information sheet indicating this fact and that, in addition, £10 was expected for the organist and £10 for the sacristan. This was by no means exorbitant when one considered what the couples had to pay photographers not to mention the hotels.

I was also chaplain to The City of Dublin Skin and Cancer Hospital, generally known as Hume Street hospital. It was founded in 1911 by Dr Andrew Charles with a number of other doctors, including his brother Frank, and was granted a royal charter in 1916. From the end of 1985 onwards it became exclusively a centre for dealing with skin diseases.

In 1983 it had 90 beds: 20 catering for skin cancer in which it specialised and 70 for patients fatally ill with that disease. My predecessor, Frank McDonnell, had established a routine satisfactory to the hospital authorities and I followed it. On Monday afternoon I visited each bed and spent some time with new arrivals. I cannot remember anyone who arrived in Hume Street hospital who was not eager to go to Confession. On Wednesday at 12 as many patients as were capable of being moved would be

brought into the largest ward and I would celebrate a short, simple Mass and add an appropriate prayer for the sick. Some of the
nurses, on their own initiative, acted as a small choir. Then on
Friday, again at noon, I would distribute Holy Communion to
all who were able to receive it.

I found the commitment and dedication of the nursing staff
most edifying. Their closeness to death caused them to be
among the most compassionate and mature people I ever met. I
administered the Last Rites / Sacrament of the anointing to those
who were terminally ill on a monthly basis. Throughout my five
years as chaplain only one person, registered as a Catholic, was
not willing to have this consoling sacrament.

Seán Comerford was one of the important assets of
University Church. He began serving Mass there in 1947 and has
been sacristan since 1959. Born locally, he was educated at Synge
Street CBS. An avid reader, his knowledge of, and attachment to
University Church is unique. Ever so gentle, kind and most
accommodating, he reminds one of a former age with his old-
world courtesy and politeness. Seán admired and forged strong
bonds of friendship with all the priests who served at University
Church.

Pat O'Kelly, a contemporary of Seán's at Synge Street CBS,
has also given sterling service to University Church. A financial
analyst at Aer Lingus and music critic for a number of news-
papers, he has acted as assistant sacristan and has supervised
the collections at the weekend Masses. I had reason to rue the closeness with which Pat supervised the collection on one occasion. I
had preached a no-holds-barred sermon on justice in general and
the reciprocal rights and duties of employers and employees in
particular. This had been prompted by two very serious strikes
which were running in tandem. The action of ESB workers and
staff had caused devastating power-cuts. Factories, commercial
enterprises, offices and homes were subjected to serial black-
outs. Farmers and especially those involved in factory-farming
in north County Dublin were grievously affected. At the same
time the national teachers were also involved in industrial

action. I pointed out the grave injustice being done to the self-employed and those employers and workers not directly involved in the disputes. I emphasised that the injustice was exacerbated by the fact that there were few other workers in the country enjoying the relatively generous pay and good working conditions and above all the job security of ESB operatives and national teachers.

Paddy Moriarty, chief executive of the ESB, and Gerry Quigley, secretary of the INTO, attended the 12 Mass every Sunday. On the Sunday in question there was no server for the 12 Mass. After taking up the collections Pat O'Kelly stood in for the server. As he handed me the water for the second ablution, he muttered: 'You bloody idiot. That sermon. We're down £20. Moriarty and Quigley put nothing in the plate for either collection.' Neither Moriarty nor Quigley returned to University Church until the strikes had been settled. Subsequently at a meeting of the Kerry Association to present the Kerry Person of the Year award I told Paddy the story. He was chairman of the Association and when presenting the award re-told the story with great gusto!

The choir which sang at the 12 Mass on Sunday was a feature of University Church. Mrs Kitty O'Callaghan was the organist and choir-mistress. An accomplished pianist, she gave recitals on the radio and in the concert hall. When I knew her, Kitty was a formidable lady, entirely different from her brother, Fr Charlie. He was the professor of Gregorian Music at St Patrick's College, Maynooth. Impeccably dressed, extremely polite and rather foppish, he seemed to me to be out of place in Maynooth which always had more the feel of a military academy than that of a major seminary. Veronica Dunne (Mrs McCarthy), the opera singer, always joined the choir on important occasions and was a popular figure around University Church.

Mrs Alice Murnaghan (1896-1999) was another person who gave a life-time of service to University Church. At the request of Fr Ned O'Brien in 1943, she undertook responsibility for the floral decoration of the altar. When I arrived at University

Church forty years later she was still discharging this responsibility with characteristic enthusiasm and style.

Alice was the widow of James A Murnaghan (1881-1973),
professor and judge and a leading member of the generation
which created the new nationalist Ireland in the early part of the
century. She was the niece of Fr Tom O'Donnell, CM, a former
president of All Hallows College, and had a number of friends
in the Vincentian Congregation. Two of her sisters were members of the Sacred Heart Order in England. She had a remarkable
interest in the well-being of her extended Davey-Murnaghan
families and was particularly close to her three brothers. Among
the younger generation her favourite, it seemed to me, was Fr
Charlie Davey SJ, then rector of Clongowes Wood College. She
fretted that he was taking the ascetic aspect of the life of a Jesuit
far too seriously!

Apart from supervising the decoration of the altar, Alice was
a staunch supporter of all other aspects of life at University
Church. The parish's returns for the five or six annual diocesan
collections for various charities were always enhanced by her
generous cheque. At her request, I brought her Holy
Communion each Saturday morning at 10.30. She always insisted
that I stay for a coffee and a chat afterwards. Although she was
in her eighties, her intellect was as sharp as ever and her memory
for her years, was truly amazing. She seemed to me to have been
one of the best-informed persons in the country at that time.
Stunningly beautiful in her youth, as was evidenced by a full-
length, colour portrait, she remained a tall, slim and elegant
lady.

Alice had a wide circle of friends belonging to several generations and presided like a great matriarch over the Davey-
Murnaghan families. Apart from news about the parish, Alice
enjoyed discussing with me details of whatever book I happened
to be preparing for publication at the time and she always
attended my book-launchings. In serial fashion she invited
members of her family from her own and then from the next
generation to come in and have lunch with her and the 'new

curate at University Church'. Lunch was simple, although very formal, in a large room and there would be in the centre of a very large table a silver object which reminded me of the mace in the House of Commons.

At that time Alice's was the only remaining privately-occupied residence in the entire Fitzwilliam Place, Square, Street area. It was also an Aladdin's cave of paintings and *objets-d'art*. The wall-space of the house, even on the stairs, was covered with impressive paintings, including Murillo's *Jacob tending the sheep of Laban*, now in the National Gallery of Ireland, an Orpen, several by early Italian masters and some seventeenth century French landscapes. I recall that a downstairs toilet had a series of line-drawings/cartoons from *Punch*. There were also valuable pieces of eighteenth century European and nineteenth century Irish furniture and eighteenth century busts. She and her late husband holidayed for many years in southern Europe. He was an art-lover and a discriminating judge of the quality and value of art of all kinds and the couple rarely returned home from their holidays without purchasing what they admired.

Alice never asked my advice on what she should do with this treasure-house of paintings and *objets-d'art*. Had she done so, I would have proposed that she set up a trust to establish a Murnaghan Memorial Museum or something along those lines in an alcove of the National Gallery of Ireland. I believed that she and her husband deserved as much. Moreover, I was in no doubt that none of her relatives or friends were in need of, or would be really better off from receiving, handsome portions of her legacy.

In the event it proved to have been a mistake to keep such a collection of valuable paintings in her house. Alice was not fully aware of how Irish society was becoming more lawless and perhaps more importantly the extent to which many people in Irish society were ceasing to have regard for moral imperatives. There was no security in the house and only a companion-housekeeper stayed with her overnight.

One Saturday morning when I arrived with Holy

Communion the distraught housekeeper told me that they had been raided by criminals. Alice, who was none the worse for the experience, was as serene as usual. I was furious when I heard her account of what happened. Four thugs entered the house at about 10 the previous night. While the others collected the items they intended to steal two of them detained Alice and her house-keeper in their respective bedrooms. One of them, brandishing a revolver, sat next to Alice who had to sit up until the small hours. At about four o'clock in the morning one of the criminals discovered an unmade bed in the house and, thinking someone might have got out of the house to alert the Gardaí, they de-camped. I asked Alice was she frightened. She replied: 'Not at all. As long as I could say my Rosary I wasn't frightened.' In my mind's eye I could see her saying Rosary after Rosary on her large, decorative set of beads.

Alice told only Eugene, her favourite brother, and me of her ordeal. She asked us to promise not to disclose anything about it to anyone, as she did not wish the family or her friends to be worrying about her safety. To no avail we pleaded with her to refer the matter to the Gardaí. The inevitable occurred. The thugs returned and stole a number of her most valuable paint-ings and other objects. Although most of the stolen goods were eventually retrieved, the ordeal was most distressing for a lady of her age.

After I left the parish, although Alice had invited me to call on her whenever I was in town, I did so on only two occasions. I regard as very wise the diocesan practice, whereby when a priest leaves a parish he leaves it. It is only fair that one's succes-sor be given space to establish himself and not have somebody getting in the way of his ministry. My return visits to Alice were occasioned by my borrowing a photograph which I required for an illustration in a publication. This was a picture of the Constitution Committee of Saorstát Éireann 1922, of which her husband was a member. On this last occasion she had become a centenarian. One of her nieces told me on the way in that she was blind. Had I not been told, I would not have noticed it from her demeanour. As elegant in appearance and movement and as well-groomed as ever, she was quite alert but very frail. As I left I felt sad, reflecting on the platitudes in Cicero's treatise on old age. But then I recalled Alice's indomitable Christian Faith and knew that her declining years and even death would pose very few difficulties for her.

During my time at University Church Dermot Ryan, then just a year into his work at the Congregation of the Propagation of the Faith in Rome, died. He had an aneurysm in the brain which left him dead in twenty minutes. His sudden and tragic death took everyone by surprise, including the press. I had a phone call from Ronan Farren at the *Evening Herald*, asking me to prepare 600 words on the late archbishop. I was delighted to oblige, not least because Ronan had been particularly helpful to me in having a number of my books reviewed. Ronan gave me two hours to have the piece with him. In due course it appeared in the *Evening Herald* of 22 February 1985.

In the meantime Bishop Kevin MacNamara of Kerry had succeeded to the see of Dublin. I was very pleased with the appointment, as I regarded Kevin as having a stature matched by few, if any, of his colleagues on the episcopal bench. I was surprised at the xenophobic comments of some of my colleagues at Kevin's appointment. He quickly silenced his critics by show-ing what an Irish archbishop could do and should do. It was heartening to see how such a gentle, diffident, mild person could show the courageous leadership which was a feature of his tenure in Dublin.

The last year of Kevin's short stewardship in Dublin was bedevilled by ill-health. A problem which he had with cancer during his time in Kerry flared up once more. His awareness of this condition had caused him to express grave reservations when he had been asked to take on the responsibility of the archdiocese of Dublin. However, his medical adviser, to Kevin's disappointment, had indicated confidence that the transfer from Kerry to Dublin would not present a medical problem. By the end of his ministry in Dublin, I had developed the same kind of admiration for Kevin as I have for Pope John Paul II. About a week before Kevin died I realised that I had never expressed solidarity with him or dropped him a note to congratulate him on his courage and steadfastness during difficult periods. In haste I sent him a note. By return of post I received what is probably one of the last, if not the last, letters he wrote – a one line scrawl of thanks – which I have since treasured.

More than a year elapsed before Des Connell was appointed to succeed Kevin MacNamara. As senior auxiliary bishop, Joe Carroll once again took charge of the archdiocese. As on a previous occasion, before MacNamara's appointment, he showed that with him the archdiocese was in safe hands. At his request I preached in the Pro-Cathedral at the meeting of the chapter on 14 November 1987, feast of St Laurence O'Toole, patron of the archdiocese.

In 1988 Dublin Corporation celebrated the city's millennium. An attractive programme of events was inaugurated with an Ecumenical Service in Christ Church cathedral on Sunday, 17 January. Bishop Joe Carroll was invited to preach the homily. Joe knew that I was interested in history and he asked me to draft a thirty-minute-long address giving an overview of the influence of Christianity on Dublin during the previous one thousand years. I did so and Joe in a characteristically effusive note of thanks told me it was very well received by the congregation. He also sent me a beautiful, coffee-table volume, written in German and English and then just published, Michael Rosenfeld's *Bundesrepublik Deutschland* (Stuttgart 1997), which had been presented to him by the German ambassador as a mark of appreciation for his homily!

In due course Des Connell was appointed archbishop. It was stated at the time that Kevin MacNamara's known very high regard for Des was a factor in his selection. As I was aware of Des' qualities of sincerity and intellect, I considered him to be an admirable choice. He has not disappointed. Unfailing in reminding his fellow priests of their primary spiritual role, he has been remarkably successful in the conduct of all aspects of the day to day running of the archdiocese during very difficult times.

Soon after Des' appointment had been announced I received a note from him asking me to draft an article on St Laurence O'Toole. He had, it seems, promised one to Fr Paul Leonard, SJ, editor of *The Sacred Heart Messenger*. I was delighted to oblige. In a gracious acknowledgement Des told me he had no need to change a word in what I sent him. In due course the article appeared over his name in *The Sacred Heart Messenger* of November 1988.

Preaching was an important aspect of the ministry in University Church and Fionán O'Sharkey and I preached at the seven Masses every second weekend. Newman was at pains to ensure that his church was suitable for preaching. Hence the ornate pulpit which is one of its features. But, following the liturgical reforms of Vatican II, in my time, except for special occasions, we preached from an ambo on the gospel side of the altar.

Many of the famous preachers of their time, such as Newman himself and his successor, Fr William Anderdon SJ, were heard in University Church. The tradition of having famous English preachers grace the pulpit at University Church was continued throughout the nineteenth and twentieth centuries. Seán Comerford and Pat O'Kelly had a remarkable appreciation and grasp of theological niceties and I profited from their positive criticism on not a few occasions. Both could be described as connoisseurs of a good sermon and they liked to reminisce on the succession of famous preachers who were invited from England to preach parish or university retreats or on other special occasions, such as the Holy Week retreat which drew extraordinary crowds to the church. On Good Friday the preacher would deliver seven sermons on the 'Last Words from the Cross' during the three hours devotion from noon to 3 o'clock. That devotion seemed to be particularly attractive to office workers planning to spend Easter with family or friends in the country: for very many of them the break started with their visit to University Church. Seán and Pat recalled memorable sermons preached by Frs Bernard Bassett, James Brodrick, James Christie, Joseph

Christie and Martin D'Arcy from the ranks of the English Jesuits; Frs Edward Coyne and John Carmel Heenan (later cardinal) of the Catholic Missionary Society and Fr Ian Hislop, OP, of Blackfriars, Oxford. Down through the years the best-known preachers from the Birmingham and Brompton Oratories also came to University Church.

Two sermons I heard in University Church, and of which I retained a vivid recollection, were radically different. The first was delivered by Mgr Ronald Knox, Catholic convert, Oxford academic and world-renowned Scripture scholar. He preached at the Mass marking the opening of the UCD students retreat in Holy Week 1953. I was a member of the Students Special Choir in Clonliffe and we were asked, under our director, Fr Bennie Lawless, to sing at the High Mass. Knox arrived on the altar with the rest of the sacred ministers. He knelt on a *priedieu* in the sanctuary, where he proceeded to read his breviary. When the time came for him to preach he laid aside his breviary and took up a folder containing his sermon. He ascended the high pulpit and in measured and rather flat tones read the twenty-five-minute-long sermon. Then he closed the folder, returned to his *priedieu* and resumed reading the Divine Office.

Some thirty-five years later different times occasioned a different style of preaching. Joe Cassidy, archbishop of Tuam, was the principal celebrant of a Mass in University Church to mark the opening of the Triennial International Conference of the Catholic press. Joe, in a sermon just as effective as that of Ronald Knox, spoke in very simple words, without notes, with a visible earnestness and for less than ten minutes.

The congregation at University Church was unusual. Only a small proportion were local residents and parishioners. Over many years, largely because of the Newman ethos of the church, people from all over the archdiocese, some from as far away as Bray, developed a habit of attending Sunday Mass in St Stephen's Green. The legal and medical profession were well represented. There was a sprinkling of academics from TCD and UCD. A number of government ministers, when overnight in Dublin, attended Sunday Mass there.

The most noticeable attender at the church was Gerry, a gentle 'man of the roads', from Castleisland. Fionán was particularly kind and generous to him. Whenever Gerry was staying in Dublin at the Salvation Army hostel nearby he always arrived for the 12 Mass on Sunday. Invariably he made a rather late entrance and carrying his possessions, generally in three, very full plastic bags, he would slowly make his way up to the front seat in the church. Every eye would be fixed on him – when preaching Fionán and I knew that the attention of the congregation was lost until he had finally put down his bags and settled in his place!

Others to catch the eye on Sunday morning were a few officials from the Canadian and US embassies who often appeared in formal dress. Then there was Lord Killanin doing his best not be noticed but failing miserably because of his physical size. He walked over from his residence in Lansdowne Road to the 11 Mass each Sunday. In appearance like a large Buddha, he always took up a central position towards the end of the church somewhat like the Speaker in the House of Commons.

One was acutely aware that the congregation expected a good sermon, but they were also most appreciative of a well-prepared homily. Because of Newman's association with the church, when appropriate I liked to include a quotation from one of his writings. On more than one occasion, to my embarrassment, Judge Declan Costello complimented me on being a Newman scholar! I recall other less fulsome compliments. On the occasion of the first referendum on Divorce I had emphasised that it was important for society's well-being that the law should be tilted in favour of stable marriage rather than the reverse. Michael Mills, the ombudsman, also a constant attender at University Church, said to me: 'Father, the trouble with you fellows is you are too good at your jobs.' Also Killanin told me on a number of occasions: 'Father, I always enjoy your sermons very much. That, however, is not to say that I agree with everything you say!'

It was not only the professional classes who attended

University Church. On one occasion, having preached on the reciprocal obligations of employers and employees, an irate gentleman came to see me. He disclosed that he was the proprietor of three small factories and that my kind of preaching made his life very difficult. After the same sermon I was approached by John Dunne and Eugene McCarthy. They were the two most senior executives in the Irish Business and Employers Confederation and they invited me to address their annual conference that autumn. I agreed and in the company of the dean of the law faculty in the University of Vienna, a director of a UK based multi-national company and Tom Toner who held directorships in six Irish companies I gave one of the four main presentations at that year's conference. I was pleasurably surprised at the generous recompense – £700 – which I received for my effort. Subsequently Fr Ronan Drury published my paper in *The Furrow* of December 1987 under the title 'The Irish work ethic'.

University Church was also a centre for the activities of the 'Friends of Cardinal Newman', a group committed to praying and working for the beatification and ultimately the canonisation of the great cardinal. In conjunction with them, Fionán organised a special Mass and sermon each October. He also cherished the library and collection of Newman memorabilia gathered by one of my predecessors, Fr Bennie Lawless, then to be seen in the interview-room of the presbytery, and took great delight in occasionally being able to add to this collection.

Another feature of University Church was the number of Americans who visited it during the summer and autumn months. Nearly all of them would be members of Newman Clubs or Newman Associations, a surprising number of which were attached to Catholic and non-Catholic colleges and universities across the US. One such visitor was Sister Madeleine Kisner, ASC. She was a Newman scholar and head of an English department in a Catholic college in the mid-west.

I met Sister Madeleine when she was examining our Newman collection. She showed me a *haiku* which she had written on the life of John Henry Newman. A *haiku* is a Japanese poetic form of three lines with seventeen syllables, five in the first and third lines and seven in the second. It was a brilliant composition. I suggested that in lieu of the homily we should present it to all the congregations over one weekend. She readily agreed. We gave advance notice of our intention and on the weekend in question provided all our Mass attendance with a copy of the *haiku*. It was presented by Sister Madeleine, Pat O'Kelly and a lady from the congregation in the manner of a 'Three Tenors' concert. It was very enthusiastically received and I was delighted to be able to pass on to Sister Madeleine some very generous cheques subsequently presented in appreciation of our efforts. Sister Madeleine gave me permission to include this *haiku* as an Appendix in *Newman's University Church: a history and guide* which I published ten years later.

As the time for the summer changes approached in 1988, I was becoming a little anxious about when I would be appointed a parish priest and what kind of parish it would be. The only other time I experienced this kind of feeling was in Maynooth, just before being informed that I was to be ordained a subdeacon. In Maynooth that was the stage at which the authorities made a final decision that students, who by that time had completed six years of intensive training, should be promoted to the priesthood.

A short time after Easter 1988 Fr Paddy Tuohy, who just then had become *Pastor Emeritus* of Rathfarnham, came into University Church to celebrate a silver jubilee Mass for a group of medical graduates. Paddy was noted for 'winding people up'. He asked me was I due to get a parish soon. I said I was and that already quite a few of my classmates had been so honoured. In fact I told him that several of those ordained after me had parishes. He asked me did I play golf. I said: 'No.' In that case he said gravely: 'I'm afraid you will be waiting for a good while more for your parish.' I told my housekeeper, Gretta, about this little humorous exchange.

In the meantime I had been collecting golf balls at a nearby petrol station. They were given free when one purchased £10

worth of petrol. I was keeping them in my car for the next golf-
playing friend who came in to conduct a marriage in University
Church. Two days after I told Gretta about the exchange with
Paddy Tuohy, a friend and keen golfer was due in for a marriage
in University Church. I lined up seven golf balls in a hall-stand
in the presbytery so as to present them to him. Gretta was out
shopping when I did this and when she arrived in and saw them
she burst into my study and said: 'Surely Father you don't have
to take up golf in order to get a parish?' With a mixture of irrit-
ation and shame-facedness I replied: 'Gretta, I'm not that des-
perate!'

CHAPTER 12

Guardian Angels', Newtownpark, Blackrock 1988-2000

In the fourth week of May 1988 there was a flurry of appointments to parishes. During the long period which elapsed between the fatal illness of Kevin MacNamara and the accession of his successor a larger than usual number of these had become vacant, owing to the deaths of the incumbents. There were also a number of parish priests who had reached the age for retirement. As soon as he had been ordained archbishop, Desmond Connell set about appointing parish priests, where this was required. Those who had reached their seventy-fifth birthday were invited to archbishop's house, where they signed back their parishes to the archbishop. Those of us who were to be appointed were also invited in. For us the situation was something of a lottery. Until the moment came none of us had any indication as to where we might be assigned. But, as was the practice at that time, we were prepared to accept responsibility for whatever parish was offered.

The archbishop told me that Fr Paddy Murray had been in an hour earlier and had resigned Guardian Angels, Newtownpark, in Blackrock. He asked me would I take responsibility for it. I replied that I would be delighted to do so and signed the required document accordingly. For me there was a curious coincidence about the date. On the same day, 26 May, I had been ordained thirty-one years earlier.

Of Newtownpark in South County Dublin Francis Elrington Ball in his *Extract from a history of the county of Dublin: Part First* (Dublin 1902) wrote:

These lands, originally known as Newtown Little, are first

mentioned at the time of the dissolution of the religious houses [and again in 1564] and there is reason to think were then the site of an ancient chapel ... In the sixteenth century the lands, on which there was a good slated house, were in the possession of the owners of Stillorgan, and were occupied by members of the Wolverston family. They continued in their possession during the next century ... As the eighteenth century advanced, villas were built and the lands became populated ...

The area now known as Newtownpark, which was part of that property with its centre in Stillorgan, was described in the title deeds as 'Deer Park'. Following the building of the 'villas', referred to by Elrington Ball, a cluster of cottages were built for the workers who served the great houses. These were initially described as the New Town in the Deer Park which title was eventually abbreviated to Newtownpark. The names of existing homes in the core section of the parish such as: 'Elm Cottage', 'Fieldview Cottage', 'Moores Cottages', 'Rose Cottage', and 'Walsh's Cottage', as well as such names as Annaville Avenue and Orchard Lane survive from the beginnings of that New Town in the Deer Park.

Newtownpark was part of Blackrock's St John the Baptist parish which itself was separated from Booterstown in 1922. When Archbishop McQuaid appointed Fr John Redmond to Blackrock in 1956 he instructed him to build a church which would have the title 'Guardian Angels' with a view to establishing a new parish. Eventually the parish was constituted from Blackrock in 1968, a year after the church was completed. This had been greatly facilitated by the Daughters of Charity of St Vincent de Paul nearby who had donated the sites for the church and the school. The new parish had 1,200 families in houses and apartments, more than half of whom had formerly belonged to Blackrock parish, the rest to that of Foxrock. Fr Willie O'Rourke was the first parish priest serving from 1968 to 1972.

Over the years the parish has developed considerably, owing to continuous house-building in the area. It now has over 2,000 families. It is one third working-class, one-third middle class and one-third upper middle-class. However, there is a signal lack of class-consciousness in the parish, the class distinctions visible only by virtue of the homes people reside in and the size of their incomes.

The first formal engagement the new parish priest has in the archdiocese of Dublin is the ceremony at which he is inducted. This ceremony which was introduced in 1972 is conducted during Mass on Sunday or on an evening during the week. In an appropriate liturgy the new incumbent is presented with the parish and accepts it. Subsequently he has an admirable opportunity to meet many of his new parishioners during a social. This is a considerable improvement on the practice which preceded it. I was present at a number of the hand-overs of parishes. The new parish priest came to the sacristy and was met by the transferred incumbent and the curates. The sacristan was also present. Then in the presence of the vicar-general the incoming parish priest recited the 'Creed' and was formally handed the keys of the church.

Fr Paddy Murray, my predecessor, was the second parish priest of Newtownpark, serving from 1972 to 1988. He was born at Templederry, County Tipperary. An excellent raconteur, he was steeped in the lore of his home place. He enjoyed reminiscing about the 'Young Irelander', Fr John Kenyon who was parish priest of Templederry for almost 25 years. Prolific contributor to *The Nation* and close friend of Charles J. Kickham, Kenyon by virtue of his patriotic fervour and oratorical gifts had an influence far beyond the boundaries of his parish. Bishop Joseph Shanahan, CSSp, the trail-blazing missionary of Nigeria, was another local hero about whom Paddy enthused. He also had a fund of stories about the 'characters' in the archdiocese in his time. He stayed on in the parish and remained very active until a year before he entered a Nursing Home. In carrying out his core priestly duties: his daily and Sunday Masses, his Saturday morning and evening Confessions, his distribution of Communion at the later Sunday Masses, his turn of preaching, his First Friday calls and systematic house visitation, he was a wonderful example to all of us.

Fr Jack Archdeacon, a native of Kanturk, was the senior curate. A gentle, cultured man, he liked to paint water-colours. He had a keen interest in modern Irish painting and had collected quite a few pictures before they had become very valuable. Unfortunately Jack had had a few strokes which left him seriously disabled. Nonetheless he manfully carried out his duties as best he could.

Fr Séamus Toohey, from Tubercurry, the father of the parish, was appointed a curate in St John the Baptist parish in Blackrock in 1967 with special responsibility for the developing area of Newtownpark. Under the direction of Canon John Redmond he acquired accommodation for the future staff of the proposed new parish, supervised the building of Guardian Angels church and was involved in the preliminary steps leading to the establishment of Scoil na nAingeal: Guardian Angels National School. He has not enjoyed the best of health. In July 1999 the British Diabetic Association awarded him the Alan Nabarro Medal in recognition of his valiant fight against diabetes for over 50 years. Yet he is the most effective colleague in pastoral terms that I have had the privilege to minister alongside. Ever encouraging I have been greatly indebted to him for his loyalty and much courtesy, kindness and help.

Fr Tim Hurley, from Kilmichael in County Cork, was the third curate. Also an excellent pastoral man, he was most popular and very happy in Newtownpark. After a brief acquaintance I developed a deep respect for his judgement. Accordingly one afternoon I arranged to meet him and asked him what changes, in the light of his ten years experience of the parish, he would make were he the new pastor.

Tim was forthright. He said the people did not know where the priests resided. I replied that within three weeks the required 'parochial house' and 'presbytery' signs would be up. He also suggested that, while it had been done some years earlier, the parish was in need of a systematic visitation. I assured him that within eight or nine months I would have called on the 2,000 families and either met them or left them my visiting card. Tim recommended a number of other elementary improvements, such as ensuring the parishioners were fully aware of what duty days and what districts each priest was responsible for. This was easily rectified. He indicated that, as was then the normal practice, Paddy Murray, as parish priest, did not have a district. I told him to draw up four districts and stated that when the other priests had selected theirs I would take responsibility for the one which had been left. In addition I told Tim to include me in the duty-day rota.

Tim also informed me that each priest preached at the Mass he celebrated and that, as a result, sometimes there was not much preaching at the early, poorly attended Masses on Sunday mornings. I told him I would propose that we preach in turn at the seven Masses each weekend. To their credit the senior men, Paddy Murray and Séamus Toohey, readily agreed to this suggestion. While the challenge was beyond Jack Archdeacon, Paddy and Séamus seemed to be rejuvenated by it.

I have always favoured this arrangement for preaching where it is possible. The benefits are: (1) it is refreshing to have a different priest each Sunday, as each one has his own distinctive approach in presenting the gospel message; (2) the voice contrast between the preacher and the celebrant is helpful to the listener and (3) the preacher invariably prepares a sermon to be aired seven times far more carefully than one preached as a one-off. Advantages also accrue to the preacher: (1) he is called upon to preach not every Sunday but every second or third Sunday; (2) by the time he has preached his sermon a few times it will have been fairly well-shaped; and (3) priests are given an opportunity to be edified and to learn from the sermons of their colleagues.

Within six months of beginning my intensive visitation of the parish I experienced two different reactions. The first was in the South County Hotel, where I was having lunch. Two of the waitresses were from the parish. One had been at home when I called, the other had not. The former introduced me to the latter saying: 'You must be the only one in the parish who has not met the new parish priest.' The second reaction occurred when I was present at a meeting in Scoil na nAingeal of the parents of the children who were being prepared for First Communion. When questions from the floor were invited a parent stood up and began to complain that the priests never visited their parishioners. I was sitting at the back of the hall and felt constrained to remind him that only four days earlier I had visited his family, had a conversation with himself in his own kitchen and had updated, with his help, the information on his family in my parish register or *Liber Status Animarum*.

Basic duties in Guardian Angels have remained unchanged since it was established in 1968 and are much the same as in all the large suburban parishes: six Masses on Sunday, four on Saturday and three Monday to Friday; Confessions on Saturday 10-12 and 6-45-7.30 pm; care of the housebound and the coverage of emergency calls. However, marriages are infrequent – only about 14 each year. Apart from the age pattern in the population, brides find the church, which seats 1,600, too large to be an appropriate setting for a marriage ceremony. There are 60 baptisms each year, only a fraction of which are preceded by the pre-Baptism service we offer. And, on average, we conduct about 50 funeral services annually.

The parish primary co-educational school, Scoil na nAingeal: Guardian Angels National School, was opened in 1970, with an enrolment of 75 pupils. It was expertly guided through its early development by its first principal, Mrs Mary O'Sullivan. In 1976, with the school enrolment at 210, Mrs O'Sullivan retired. She was succeeded by Tom Garry. With the new principal came a new extension to the school, consisting of an extra four classrooms and a general purposes hall: all completed in 1978. Among a number of imaginative innovations, Tom Garry organised an annual school Mass which featured the Artane Boys Band. In 1995 Tom was succeeded by Walter Cullinane and since then the school enrolment has steadily risen to 430. The highlight of Walter's principalship is the completion of the beautiful new extension formally opened by the minister for education, Mícheál Martin, TD, in 1999. This replaced the original school opened in 1970 which consisted of a pre-fabricated structure with six classrooms, a staff room and toilets.

In 1988 I succeeded Paddy Murray as chairman of the Board of Management. At the handover Paddy, who was greatly indebted to the other members, as I subsequently was, provided everyone with strawberries and cream. I remarked that I now realised that I had arrived among the 'yuppies'. Tim Hurley was acting as chaplain to both Guardian Angels National School and the Presentation Convent School at Rockford Manor. To enable him to spend more time in the latter school I took responsibility for the chaplaincy of Guardian Angels school. Each week I taught Religious Knowledge to a different class, concentrating on the ten commandments and the common prayers.

The Presentation Convent School for girls at Rockford Manor was the other important Catholic educational institution in the parish. This also owed its origin to Archbishop John Charles McQuaid. In the early 1950s he requested the Presentation Sisters to open a day secondary school in the area. As they looked around for a suitable location, Rockford Manor came on the market. Built prior to 1843 by Sir William Betham, the Ulster King of Arms at Dublin Castle, later occupied by William Bruce, Lieutenant Colonel Hume Dudgeon and still later by John Higgins, it was eventually owned by Dún Laoghaire Corporation. The Sisters bought the house and property in 1958 and a year later opened their school with 30 pupils.

A new secondary school was completed and opened in 1972, at which time the school had 300 pupils at preparatory and 400 at secondary level. Owing to a gradual decline in pupil numbers, the Sisters finally phased out their preparatory school in 1986. Then in 1989, mainly due to a shortage of Sisters available for service in schools, the Order handed over management of the school to a Board of Management, on which the Sisters are represented. Mrs Rosemary Mitchell was appointed the first lay principal in 1992. Some Sisters continued to teach in the school until 1994, when they eventually evacuated their convent. Under the new administration the school, with some 400 pupils, continues to flourish and, in the authentic educational tradition of the Presentation Sisters, provides a Christian environment where learning and teaching nurture the personal development of every student.

From the outset a member of Guardian Angels parish staff acted as chaplain to the Presentation Convent School at Rockford Manor. When Tim Hurley was transferred in 1990 and replaced by Fr Eoin Murphy I handed responsibility for Guardian Angels National School to Eoin and replaced Tim as chaplain at Rockford Manor. The Sisters and lay teachers were most supportive not least Tim Nelligan, who was the principal teacher of Religious Knowledge. With Tim's help I was able to teach a different class each week and through the year visited all 18 classrooms. I also celebrated the occasional class-Mass in the school's beautiful chapel. On one occasion an over-enthusiastic Sister encouraged her charges to bake unleavened bread for a class Mass. It was not a successful experiment! Consuming all the consecrated bread proved to be quite a challenge. Before the end of the first and second terms, with the help of colleagues from my own and adjacent parishes, I enabled all the girls to go to Confession for Christmas and Easter. Then there was the end of the year Special Mass in which we prayed that the girls would be successful in their examinations. During my time as chaplain, from 1990 to 1994, I became acutely aware that the teaching of Religious Knowledge in our schools was not satisfactory. There were many reasons for this but I considered the main fault lay in the catechetical programmes the teachers were requested to present.

The priests of the parish serve two other institutions, namely, two nursing homes: the first at Newtownpark House, the second at 'Charleville' on Newtownpark Avenue. Built in 1770, Newtownpark House was purchased by Henry Samuel Close, a banker, in 1839. It remained in the possession of his family until 1908 when it passed to the Burtons. Senator Edward A.

McGuire, proprietor of Brown Thomas's in Grafton Street, Dublin, purchased it in 1946. A much talented and flamboyant character he had his own nine-hole golf course laid out in the grounds. In 1984 when he took up residence elsewhere the property came on the market. The grounds were developed into the housing estates of Mount Albany and Richmond. After standing idle for a number of years the house was purchased by the Keane family, who, after refurbishing it extensively, had it opened as a nursing home in 1987. A new extension was completed in 1990, bringing the total provision for occupancy of the nursing home to 62 residents, as well as 14 retirement bungalows.

The second nursing home is at 'Charleville' on Newtownpark Avenue which was built about 1800. It has generally about 15 in residence. Fr Séamus Toohey, on behalf of the parish, acts as chaplain to both nursing homes, celebrating Mass at least once a week in each, frequently visiting the residents and being available on request. Such is the dedication of Séamus that neither I nor any of his other colleagues have scarcely ever had to deputise for him.

The passage of time brought the inevitable succession of departures and arrivals. When Jack Archdeacon died in 1993 he was succeeded by Fr Bernard Collier who in turn was replaced by Fr Con Sayers. After serving as parish priest for less than two years I met Bishop Dermot O'Mahony. Unknown to me he was at the time casting around for an able and experienced curate to fill a vacancy in Rush, then a challenging appointment. Rather naively I trumpeted the qualities of the staff at Newtownpark in general and those of Tim Hurley in particular. Very soon afterwards Tim was transferred to the then difficult curacy in Rush. He was replaced by Fr Eoin Murphy who in turn gave way to Fr Pat Sheehan. Eventually Pat was replaced by Fr Cyril Mangan.

Cyril arrived in the parish by a happy coincidence. He served as chief chaplain of the St Joseph's Young Priests Society from 1988 to 1993. This Society for the promotion of the Catholic priesthood, diocesan and religious, at home and abroad, began in 1895 with the publication of the quarterly *St Joseph's Sheaf*. In that year the Society financed the education of two Irish boys who wished to serve as priests in China and the Far East. By 1923 the Society was paying for the education of 32 boys in various Irish colleges. The annual report of the Society for 1993 recorded that it was financing the education of 764 seminarians, 103 of whom had been ordained that summer. This was achieved by the development by the Society from a 'Drawing-room meeting of workers for the apostolic students of St Joseph' in 1895 to an organisation of 439 branches with some 100,000 members who contributed almost one million pounds to the Society in 1993.

Strange as this may seem, although I had heard of the name of the Society, I knew little else about it. Then in 1991 Mrs Kathleen Reynolds, a member of the executive committee of the Society, called on me. She asked me to help her establish a branch in the parish. After a briefing on the aims and work of the Society I was most enthusiastic to do so. At Fr Toohey's suggestion, I canvassed parishioners who were relatives of priests, as well as others whom I judged would be suitable for membership. A meeting was arranged which was addressed by Kathleen. We were all impressed by her earnestness. A branch was established which continues to flourish and each year, apart from its spiritual activities, it contributes an average of £1,000 to the St Joseph's Young Priests Society.

Subsequently I learned that Kathleen's sterling efforts and those of her colleagues to establish new branches in parishes was one of the projects undertaken by them in preparation for the celebration of the Society's centenary. This had been prompted by a decline in the membership of vocational branches, such as those in the banks, civil-service, motor-trade, vintner trade, etc. It was also occasioned by a new awareness of how crucially important the work of the Society was becoming in the face of obvious signs of the dramatic decline of vocations in Ireland. Another contemporary project the Society undertook was to have a definitive biography of Olivia Mary Taaffe, their foundress, published. On behalf of the executive committee, Cyril asked me to prepare the biography. I replied that when I had finished a work in hand I would most gladly do so.

In due course *Olivia Mary Taaffe (1832-1918): Foundress of St Joseph's Young Priests Society* (Dublin 1995) was launched by Cardinal Cahal Daly in the beautifully refurbished head office of the Society. I felt greatly honoured in being able to reciprocate in this way the outstanding service given to the Catholic priesthood by members of the Society. I was also very pleased to help with some of the Society's other centenary events. Guardian Angels church was the venue for the Society's Dublin centenary celebration and I attended as a Dublin delegate the national celebration at Knock. And I was the main speaker at the Society's annual national congress in the centenary year. In my dealings with the Society I met Cyril Mangan frequently and on one occasion jokingly suggested that he should join me in Newtownpark at least to improve the age profile of the staff. This he did and much more.

I was made uncomfortably aware of the difference between Cyril's age and that of the rest of us on the staff on one occasion. Cyril, like his peers, is very partial to new trends in spirituality! For the most part I do not discourage him in this matter and we have had presentations from a number of those articulating these modern trends. One of these consisted in the establishment of Basic Christian Communities. After Cyril assured me that these would be a major benefit to the parish, I replied, I must confess, rather wearily: 'All right. Let's have them.' I then asked him to tell me something about the priest who would be helping him to set them up. He told me he was Fr Jim O'Halloran, that he was a Salesian residing in the Order's house in Crumlin, that Jim lectured on this and cognate subjects in the Milltown Park theologate, that he had first-hand experience of Basic Christian Committees as a missionary in Uganda and then Cyril added: 'He's elderly. He's about sixty'! I flinched, suddenly very conscious of my age.

The parishioners are the outstanding asset of Newtownpark.

From the beginning I set out to build on their readiness to take responsibility for different aspects of parish activity. The result is some 30 committees or groups who organise and supervise activity right across the parish. In delivering the Dublin Diocesan Jubilee 2000 programme to the homes of the parish we included an insert setting out the services provided by the parish and a list of its active committees and groups. The latter were described as follows:

> Adoration of the Blessed Sacrament Group, Altar Servers, Altar Society, Basic Christian Community, Board of Management Scoil na nAingeal, Bookshop Team, Catholic Boy Scouts, Choir/Senior & Junior, Church Cleaners, Church Collectors/Indoor & Outdoor, Eucharistic Ministers, Lay Carmelite Prayer Group, Legion of Mary, Liturgy Group, Marian Shrine Group, Millennium Group, Newsletter Editors, Parish Advisory Council, Parish Finance Committee, Pre-baptism Group, Readers, Sacristans, St Joseph's Young Priests Society, St Vincent de Paul Conference and Senior Citizens Group.

In canvassing support for these committees and groups I try to ensure that as many people as possible become involved. Thus over 300 different persons belong to them. One very important practical benefit from this remarkable commitment to voluntary service is that the parish does not have any paid staff, apart from the priests. Even the annual accounts are audited on a voluntary basis. All the groups joined with great gusto in celebrating our various jubilees: the silver jubilee of the church in 1992, Fr Murray's diamond jubilee in 1996 and Fr Toohey's golden jubilee in 1999.

Every parish has its complement of unsung heroes and heroines. At Newtownpark there were three who I regarded as having been outstanding in their service of the parish and I was delighted to be able to acknowledge the gratitude of their fellow parishioners by having them awarded the papal *Bene Merenti* medal.

Mrs Ita McGarry received the medal in 1994. For more than

twenty years she had been helping the sacristan or acting as sacristan in the church. Apart from a myriad of other services provided by Ita, she and her husband, Jack, opened and closed the church daily for some twenty years.

Bob Doyle, who received his *Bene Merenti* medal in 1993, was born locally and educated at Dún Laoghaire Christian Brothers School. In the Marian Year of 1957, with other residents in Marian Park, he received permission from the County Council to build a Marian Shrine on a waste piece of ground. This initiative was prompted by the Sisters of Mercy. They had handed over to the Health Authority the administration of Cluan Mhuire, then as now a centre for the treatment of those suffering from mental health problems. In the changeover a beautiful metal statue of Our Lady, which stood at the entrance to Cluan Mhuire, had to be removed and the Sisters donated it to the Marian Park residents. Since the erection of the statue Bob and some of his neighbours have carefully maintained the beautiful Shrine. Bob also has always been a key-figure in fund-raising and in supervising the various parish collections and, with his wife May, he has been an indefatigable worker in the Senior Citizens Group for over twenty years.

Denis Murray, who also attended Dún Laoghaire Christian Brothers School, was conferred with the *Bene Merenti* medal in 1993. A rate-collector, peace commissioner and friend and staunch supporter of Liam Cosgrave, former TD and Taoiseach, he was most active in Blackrock parish and since its establishment in Guardian Angels parish. Most obliging and generous to a fault with his time, he has been and continues to be a key-figure in fund-raising and the supervision of church collections. Since 1985, when required, he has acted as an assistant sacristan. In 1989 I appointed him parish co-ordinator and since then he has solved for me and the other priests quite a few administrative problems. One can gather the measure of Denis's commitment from an incident which occurred in 1992. Immediately after the Sunday evening Mass a gang of thugs arrived and conducted a carefully planned robbery. Denis was struck with a hammer, seriously injured and had to be taken into intensive care. Notwithstanding this, he was back giving most of his waking hours to the parish in less than a month.

In the spring of 1990 Archbishop Connell organised a diocesan Eucharistic renewal programme. Those who prepared the materials for the programme assumed it would be presented at meetings on week nights over the period. In Newtownpark we considered it would be regrettable if the entire parish had not an opportunity to benefit from the programme. Thus we presented it at the most popular Masses on each of the Sundays during the period in question. It was very well received. I prepared a report on it which was published in *Link-Up* of July 1990 and in *The Furrow* of July-August 1990. This report is printed in Appendix 3.

Every parish priest very soon realises that his most onerous responsibility is ensuring the financial viability of the parish and attending to the maintenance of the church or churches, centre/hall, schools and presbyteries. When I arrived in Newtownpark in 1988 the parish debt was £60,000. This was mostly the residue of the debt incurred in 1967 by the initial provision of the church, primary school and three presbyteries. The outdoor collection – so called because it is taken up not in church but right across the parish – realised £40,000 annually. This outdoor collection meets the parish's running expenses and helps to reduce the overall parish debt. Because of the continuing size of the debt in Newtownpark much needed maintenance had had to be postponed.

A veteran of three planned-giving campaigns, I had little enthusiasm for launching into another one, but it had to be done. The model for these campaigns was provided by an English firm of financial consultants, named 'Wells'. Anglican in origin, they were invited into the archdioceses in 1960 to add professional 'know how' to fund-raising in parishes. With the help of the judicious advice of my colleagues who knew Newtownpark parish so well, I painstakingly put in place a parish finance committee and more importantly an outdoor collection committee. The members of these excellent committees conducted an intensive

house to house canvass of the entire parish. Over 60% of parishioners pledged or promised to pledge to contribute to the
re-vamped outdoor collection. In the event only 35% of those
pledges were honoured. However, the collection rose to £60,000
annually and has remained steady at that figure ever since.

The establishment of the Dublin Diocesan Finance Secretariat
greatly reduced financial pressures on parish priests. Its success
is due in no small measure to the manner in which Mgr John
Wilson ably presides over it, as did his predecessor Mgr
Desmond Williams. Nonetheless, like any other parish priest, I
have to spend time at the beginning of each month carefully
checking bank statements, in my case reports on six accounts.

In the autumn of 1988 I had a visit from Mary Keating, a lecturer in the department of industrial relations, in the faculty of
commerce in UCD. At the time Mary was teaching on a two-year
course leading to an MBA (Master of Business Administration)
for business executives. The 30 persons taking the course included
potential 'high-fliers' selected from the various commercial and
State companies. At that particular time the question of the relationship between ethics and business had come to the fore. The
credibility of the management of the New York stock exchange
was being undermined by allegations and revelations concerning the extensive insider-dealing of Jan Boski. At home there
was growing disquiet about the conduct and *modus operandi* of
company directors following investigations into malpractices
allegedly pursued by Ernest Saunders of the Guinness Co and
others. As a result, Mary decided that the course she was supervising should have an input on ethics.

I was taken aback when Mary, who knew me because she,
her husband and children attended University Church, asked
me to conduct a seminar on ethics and business for her students.
Helpless in the face of flattery, I agreed. In preparing for the
seminar I re-visited a text-book on ethics and my theological
tract *De Justitia*: *On Justice*. And Mary gave me a collection of articles from journals published by Schools of Business Studies in
the US. As I prepared I became uneasy about one particular

issue and spent a disproportionate amount of time reading-up on it and reflecting on it. At the time the practice of the Catholic Church in restricting ordination to men was a favourite topic of feminists and of the clerical chattering classes. Mary had told me that eight of her students were women. I anticipated an objection to my pontificating on justice when my institution/company discriminated against women with regard to ordination/employment. My reticence on this issue was not owing to my unwillingness to discuss it but I felt that it could get in the way of dealing with other issues more pertinent to business students. Also in discussing this and cognate issues I have a horror of appearing to be unchivalrous.

In the event the seminar went well and I greatly enjoyed the exchange with the students. The issue of women priests did not come up. At the end Mary summarised the proceedings and Professor Michael McCormac came along to thank me. In a few closing remarks I indicated my anxiety about the topic of women priests and my relief that it had not been raised and left!

In the spring of 1994 I was asked by Cecil Hurwitz to preach at a Mass for Industrial Peace in St Mary's Dominican church in Cork. The Mass, held on the third Sunday of October, had been organised annually by Cecil since 1979. At the Mass employees and employers, employers' organisations – industrial and agricultural – and the trade-union movement were invited to pray for industrial peace and employment.

To introduce himself Cecil sent me his autobiography, *From synagogue to church* (Cork 1991). It told a fascinating story. In 1884 Cecil's father and other Lithuanian Jews boarded a ship for the US. However, they were disembarked in Ireland and settled in Cork forming the core of that city's Jewish community. Cecil was born in 1926, received a traditional Jewish upbringing, was later educated by the Presentation Brothers and eventually began to study medicine at UCC. While at university his conversion to Catholicism, although not as sudden, was as dramatic as St Paul's conversion on the road to Damascus.

Cecil did not complete his medical studies but after a series

of jobs returned to UCC in his early forties and qualified as a sec-
ondary-school teacher, a profession he followed until he retired.
A dedicated ecumenist throughout his life, he was deeply affected
by the conflict in Northern Ireland and became involved in an
organisation called P.E.A.C.E. (Prayer, Enterprise and Christian
Effort) which had been established to promote peace and reconciliation in Ireland. From 1977 onwards he organised a Cork
Peace Week in which the leaders of the major churches in Cork
enthusiastically joined. Later, with others, he formed the Cork
Peace Council which arranged holidays in Youghal for Catholic
and Protestant families from Northern Ireland.

In due course I preached at the Mass for Industrial Peace.
Cecil had quite a flair for publicity and I was somewhat abashed
when I saw the huge posters advertising the event and announc-
ing that I was to address the annual gathering. I was amazed at
the support for this Mass. It was almost like a civic occasion.
Apart from the presence of the Catholic and Church of Ireland
bishops and other religious representatives, it was attended in
their robes by the lord mayor and the other members of the
Corporation, as well as representatives of trade-unions, employers' groups and practically every other public body active in
Cork's civic life. When I was in Cork Cecil proudly showed me
the *Bene Merenti* medal with which he had been conferred for his
work for peace. I had a few long conversations with him and
was impressed at the extent and depth of his knowledge of the
Faith and its Biblical origins.

In recent years, initially at the request of the management of
the Doyle Tara Hotel, I have provided Mass for the Kerry football team when they play in Dublin. I take a school-boy delight
in this! It involves having dinner with the management and
team on the previous evening and celebrating Mass in the hotel
at 10.30 on Sunday morning. On these occasions I have great difficulty in restraining myself from straying beyond my brief. I
have very strong views on what I regard as the match-losing
style of play adopted by Kerry teams during the past decade.
Nobody perhaps is in a better position to testify to this than the

gentlemanly Denis Moran, former team manager and representative of the South-West Regional Tourism Authority, whom I have harangued year after year when meeting him at Writers Week, Listowel. At this stage the much put-upon Paudie O'Shea is probably also finding me somewhat tiresome on the subject.

The annual retreats for the priests are one of the most unchanging features of life in the archdiocese. They are held in the third and fourth weeks in June. Two retreat directors are invited to conduct them. The two sessions of the first retreat are held concurrently, one in All Hallows College and the other in Clonliffe College and two sessions of the second take place similarly during the second week. An average of 150 priests attend each session.

The second retreat, in All Hallows College, is known as 'Rural Week' because for many years it has been reserved for the majority of the priests serving in County Dublin, nearly all of County Wicklow and in parts of Counties Kildare and Wexford. From early on I found this retreat most congenial and whenever possible opted for it. It has a distinctive air of casualness and relaxation which those ministering in the country bring to it.

Each retreat continues from Sunday evening until lunch-time on Thursday. For the most part the retreat-directors are well chosen. Unfailingly they emphasise at the first conference that they are merely instruments and that the real work of the retreat is something we have to look to ourselves. They stress the importance of keeping silent, apart from meal-times, to allow us to respond to the promptings of the Holy Spirit. To their credit, a minority of my colleagues manage to do so throughout the retreat. However, many of us give up after a day or two. I must confess that it is the spirit of conviviality rather than the Holy Spirit which looms largest during most of my retreats.

I always enjoy the company of about 180 of my colleagues. Some I would not have met for anything from five to ten years. The retreat provides an opportunity to become acquainted with the newly-ordained priests who come into the archdiocese each year. After a few days one spends time getting to know the names of the fresh-faced, young priests appearing for the first time in the opposite choir-stalls.

On one occasion as I looked across I saw five of those new 'recruits' in a row. Such was the abundance of their hair one could just about see their faces. They reminded me of a bunch of groupies who might be following around after the 'Beatles', then at the height of their popularity. To a young priest next to me I said: 'Who are they?' He told me their names and where they were ministering. The last one's Christian name was Dave. He told me he was serving in Seán McDermott Street and added: 'The teenagers call him "Dave the Rave".' 'O my God', I said, 'I know we have survived Gibbon's *The decline and fall of the Roman Empire* but I wonder will we survive this.'

The retreat gives one an opportunity to meet the 'characters'. I loved to meet Fr Jack Whelan. Jack was always in great demand for giving retreats in the various army barracks, to the inmates of Mountjoy and other prisons, and to large men's sodalities. It seems he called a spade a spade. To someone like me, over twenty years his junior, he would be quite avuncular and share his fund of interesting anecdotes and experiences. I suspected he enjoyed his reputation as a 'hard man'. This arose in part from stories about his involvement in a notorious poker school, where alarmingly high stakes were played for.

Jack was not beyond a little histrionics in the pulpit. On the occasions of the six annual major charity-collections in the arch-diocese he would speak at length on the subject of the collection and then call the chief collector up to the pulpit, ostentatiously take £10 from his wallet and give it to him. This and the great cross-section of people who attended his 9 o'clock Mass on Sunday probably accounted for the remarkably generous returns for these major collections from the parish of Sts Michael and John in the city centre. I told Jack that none of the rest of us would dare begin a collection as he did lest we be pelted with coins by members of the congregation!

Fr Joe Drumgoole, classmate and life-long friend, is another constant attender of 'Rural Week'. Always on stage and spraying irreverent comments in all directions, Joe is ever alert to put down any manifestations of pomposity.

Over the years the priests of the archdiocese have had the privilege of attending many memorable retreats. Among the most memorable for me were those conducted by Mgr Fulton Sheen and the brilliant German theologian, Fr John Fullenbach. In the case of the retreat given by Fulton Sheen we were like a studio audience. The retreat was taped to produce a disc and a video for commercial distribution. The American had his best years behind him at the time but both the content and present-ation of his talks were most impressive. He also had a remarkable physical presence. We also had in recent years interesting retreats from prelates associated with the archdiocese of Westminster: Cardinal Basil Hume, his successor, Archbishop Cormac Murphy-O'Connor, and at an earlier time Auxiliary Bishop Christopher Butler who then was a panel member of Fredie Greiswood's ground-breaking 'Any questions' programme on the BBC.

During the retreats the archbishop of the day comes to present his state of the archdiocese message. Archbishop John C. McQuaid seemed to be very ill at ease when doing so. His talk by virtue of its content and its characteristically succinct presentation was always worth listening to. But for those who were not close to him it was well-nigh impossible to hear him. He spoke rapidly and in a tone just louder than a whisper. Invariably, as I strained my ears to hear him, I recalled a story told me by a colleague.

Press representatives had been invited to archbishop's house for announcements and briefings in connection with the Patrician Congress of 1961. The proceedings were opened by John Charles. After he had spoken for about a minute an American journalist stood up and said: 'Archbishop, we can't hear you. Could you speak a little louder, please?' McQuaid glared at her and continued. At the reception afterwards the American complained to my friend that she had not been able to hear anything the archbishop said and added: 'It's alright for you guys. It seems you can lip-read.'

In January 1997 Fr Kevin Donlon, editor of *Intercom*, asked me to interview Mgr Andrew Cusack at All Hallows College. Cusack was in Dublin to make preparations for a course in clergy formation at All Hallows in the following June. A typical, outgoing American priest, he had been directing formation courses for ten years and his commitment to this ministry was unmistakeable. He stressed the importance of continuing education for priests by quoting freely from John Paul II's *Pastores Dabo Vobis*: I shall give you pastors. This emphasised that 'permanent formation is a requirement of the priest's own faithfulness to his ministry' and integral to ensuring that he deliver the best possible service of which he is capable. Cusack had a refreshing attitude to the present serious decline in vocations in the Western world, which I readily applauded. For him the solution to this problem did not lie in looking back nostalgically to the past nor dwelling on gloomy prognoses for the future. Rather it was for the priests of today to show by their dedicated service how essential they are to ensure a better world.

Cusack confidently asserted that any priest who spent an hour in prayer before the Blessed Sacrament each day would never lose his way. That set me thinking about my own prayer life. I was only too aware that it was an area where I do not score highly. True enough since ordination I have managed to celebrate Mass daily, apart from times when confined to bed with illness or finding myself in places on vacation where it was not possible even to attend Mass. On becoming a subdeacon I committed myself to the daily recitation of the Divine Office and ever since I have found it a great source of encouragement and serenity. However, I seldom pray it with the care and reverence I should. Before laying aside my breviary each day I like to recite the beautiful prayer for priests composed by St Thérèse of Lisieux:

O Jesus Eternal Priest keep these Thy servants within the shelter of Thy Heart, where none may harm them.
Keep unstained their anointed hands, which daily touch Thy Sacred Body.

Keep unsullied the lips purpled with Thy Precious Blood.
Keep pure and unearthly their hearts, sealed with the sublime marks of Thy glorious Priesthood.
Let Thy holy love surround them and shield them from the
world's contagion.
Bless their labour with abundant fruit, and may the souls to
whom they minister be here below their joy and consolation,
and in heaven their beautiful and everlasting crown.
Amen.

Apart from the official prayer of the church I like simple prayers:
the Angelus, the grace before and after meals and the Rosary.
But, despite many beginnings, I have never been able to sustain
spending a full half-an-hour in prayer and meditation before or
after my daily Mass.

As a young priest I noted that an older priest, a relative, almost
invariably ended a conversation with: *'Oremus pro invicem:* Let
us pray for each other.' Many years later I came across part of an
address by Fr Karl Rahner, SJ, at an ordination. It emphasised
how much priests are in need of the prayers and support of their
brothers and sisters in Christ:

> A priest is not an angel sent from Heaven. He is a man chosen
> from among men. This means that we priests are just as
> human as you are, not a shade different, not a bit better, poor,
> weak weary men in need of God's mercy. The darkness of the
> world darkens our minds too; we travel the same road you
> travel, out of darkness into God's light.
> We priests are men, we remain poor sinners. So we beg you
> let us bear your brotherly company along the road of life, to
> speak God's word to you and to give you God's grace.
> There is so much chatter in the world, and there are many
> clever, shallow words in the world, but I ask you, my brothers
> and sisters, have we not a crying need for someone to speak
> to us of God, of eternal life and of grace, of sin, of judgement,
> and of God's mercy? Is that still not the most important
> message today? What more can a man want?

What greater and holier mission can he have than speaking God's word to his brothers and sisters? So on such a day as this, we priests can only ask – Pray for us.

Accept God's word and holy sacramental mysteries from us. If we are bound together, priests and people, then we already bear veiled in our midst, Jesus Christ, His grace and eternal life. Amen.

CHAPTER 13

A Final Retrospect
2000

The world of 2000 is very different from the world of 1950. Not surprisingly the church has changed considerably over that period also. In 1950 the church world-wide was composed of tightly-knit communities and parishes. Members were certain of the commandments of God and of the church. They were loyal, even deferential, to church leadership. People were marked by their Catholic Faith and were clearly proud of it in public as well as in private. Today the church in the Western world can no longer be described in these terms. It has suffered from a decline in vocations, a lurch towards secularism, the growth of 'loyal dissent' and what can only be described as a congenital defensiveness with regard to our Faith.

The difficulties facing the church in the Western world have been replicated in Ireland, particularly in the last decade of the twentieth century. There is a noticeable lessening of Faith among Irish people. Signs of this are not difficult to discern. Among the most dramatic are a fall-off in religious practice, although it still remains much better than other European countries, a decline in vocations and widely-publicised scandals in which prominent and not so prominent members of the clergy and laity have been involved. It seems that Irish people are no longer a 'Faith people' in the way that most of them had been for over 150 years.

Some ascribe these developments to the Vatican Council of 1962-6. This is difficult to sustain. The major reforms of the Council: the collegiality of the bishops, the support for ecumenism, the recognition of the rights of the individual conscience, dialogue with non-Christians, the change of the liturgy from Latin into the vernacular and the encouragement of the laity, especially to exercise leadership in the world: are splendid sign-posts for the church of the present and the future. However, it is true that some well-intentioned persons, claiming Vatican II as their inspiration, have introduced changes and disruptions never intended nor even anticipated by the fathers of that great council.

It would take a skilled sociologist to outline and finesse the many, varied, inter-related and subtle causes for the lessening of faith among Irish people today. But three factors seem to be paramount: affluence, the influence of the media and the unsatisfactory nature of catechetical programmes in the pulpit and in the school.

The negative effect material prosperity can have on religious practice is well-known. One need but recall Christ's use of the image of the camel and the eye of a needle. The fact that today Ireland is one of the wealthier countries in the world is something, of which we can all be proud, the more so since for so long we have been denigrated as being a lazy and incompetent people. However, it must be admitted that prosperity can have its downside.

So omnipresent is the media in today's world that it is difficult even to begin to measure its influence. Startling advances in media technology have long since far superseded the predictions with which Marshall McLuhan amazed the world almost 40 years ago. Although the media outlets are mere instruments, those who operate them are generally influenced by the secularist ethos of the State and the consumerist philosophy of the world of business and commerce. As a result, apart from some exceptions, those who work in the media tend at best to be unsympathetic and at worst hostile to the voice of the church.

There is clear evidence that a generation of Irish people today are far less informed on the tenets of their faith than their predecessors. This must call into question the methodology used in presenting the faith in pulpit and in school over the past 30 years. For far too long the homily/sermon devoid of doctrine

and the religious knowledge period in school with an inade-
quate treatment of the teaching of Christ have been the norm.
This is one area where those of us who love the church in its
founder and as an institution and wish to advance its mission
can have an impact. A practical and essential step we could take
is to ensure that our preaching and the religion teaching in our
schools are firmly based on, and reflect, the *Catechism of the
Catholic Church* which was published in 1994 specifically for this
purpose.

An overview of the last two millennia indicates that tension
between the church and the secular world never wanes nor is
there ever a time when the church is not facing grave difficulties.
In the last century the church confronted the militant atheism
and the de-humanising of men and women associated with
communism and fascism. Today it faces an amalgam of confused
and confusing materialistic philosophies. Nor are internal dis-
sensions ever lacking in the church. Here I must confess having
considerable sympathy on the one hand with church leadership,
one of whose main responsibilities is to ensure orthodoxy of
belief, and on the other with theologians, whose task is to clothe
the unchanging teaching of Christ in the language of the present.

No one should be surprised at the tension which exists
between Church and State. The church in embodying and pro-
claiming the teaching of its founder has always been, is and
always will be a challenge to the secular world and its values.
The priest is in the forefront of that challenge. Few priests are
ever unaware of that role, of the heavy burden it can impose, of
the high demands it makes and the even higher ideals it re-
quires. I recall how many of us in the class of 1957 had printed
on our ordination cards Lacordaire's description of the priesthood:

> To live in the midst of the world without desiring its plea-
> sures; to be a member of each family yet belonging to none;
> to share all suffering; to penetrate all secrets; to heal all
> wounds; to go from men to God and offer Him their prayers;
> to return from God to men to bring pardon, peace and hope;

to have a heart of fire for charity and a heart of bronze for chastity; to teach and to pardon, to console and to bless always; this life is yours, O Priest of Jesus Christ!

For my part I have always found the priesthood very challenging but also rewarding beyond all my expectations.

All-Ireland Junior Football Final
1954

In the summer of 1954 I had played matches on practically every Sunday: with Listowel Emmets in the North Kerry League, Listowel Geraldines (a divisional team) in the Kerry County Championship and the Kerry junior team in the All-Ireland series. It was a good year for Kerry football: the senior, junior and minor teams reached the All-Ireland finals. In the event, the seniors lost to an unfancied Meath side and the minors were pipped by Dublin. The junior team, however, won an All-Ireland, not least because of the displays of the two veterans on the team: Eddie Dowling at full-forward and Tom Spillane (father of the footballing brothers Mick, Pat and Tom) at full-back.

That September students returned a week earlier to Clonliffe than they did to Maynooth. As I and the rest of the Kerry junior team were being ferried from Barry's Hotel to Croke Park for the All-Ireland final against Donegal, we passed some of my former classmates in their striking sopranos and Roman hats on their way back to Clonliffe from the Pro-Cathedral, where they had assisted at the high Mass at noon.

Confraternity of the Immaculate Conception and St Joseph

The Confraternity of the Immaculate Conception and St Joseph was established by Archbishop John Charles McQuaid in a number of parishes in 1941. In St Joseph's parish at the outset it had twenty-five members/brothers, including an estate agent, three shopkeepers, the driver of the Belfast Enterprise train and others employed in firms around the area. Their function was to recite five offices per week, lead the Rosary every weekday in the church at 7.45 pm, to assist the clergy with church collections and especially to help with stewarding, as at that time the temporary church would be full to the door. Members took an oath of allegiance to carry out these functions. Hubert Fuller, a long-standing member of the confraternity, who organised a juvenile sodality and soccer street league, was ably assisted by Fr Larry Redmond in later years. To play in the league one had to be a member of the sodality. Many well-known players emerged from this street league, including Liam Tuohy and Noel Peyton, the Irish international players (information from William Dee, member of the confraternity 1941-1999).

Reflections Arising from the
Dublin Diocesan Renewal Programme

by J. Anthony Gaughan

Inevitably the attempt to implement the diocesan Eucharistic Renewal Programme prompts some reflections. Those who conceived and prepared the programme are to be commended. The liturgical and scriptural material supplied to parishes was most useful. It was sensible that an indication was given that the material supplied was intended as an aid rather than as a programme to be carried out in detail, as at parish level flexibility is all-important.

In Newtownpark parish it was decided to present the programme to the Sunday Mass congregations. To this end, Rev Professor Thomas Marsh of St Patrick's College, Maynooth, Fr J. A. Gaughan, Fr Séamus Toohey, Rev Professor Frederick Jones, CSsR, Fr Eoin Murphy and Fr Patrick Murray lectured on the Eucharist on the six weekends from 3-4 March to 14-15 April (excluding Palm Sunday). The lectures were given at the Masses with the highest attendances, each lecturer addressing the 7 pm. Vigil Mass on Saturday and the 10, 11, 12 and 7 pm Masses on Sunday. The Sunday Mass extras were kept short and the talks averaged 20 to 25 minutes. Professor Marsh based his talk on the one which he had given to the priests of the archdiocese, stressing the real presence in the Eucharist and the notion of sacrifice in the Mass. Fr Gaughan's treatment was based on the Eucharistic discourses in the gospel of St John. In his presentation Professor Jones illustrated the relevance of the Sunday Eucharist in the lives of those who would wish to be followers of Christ. Fathers Toohey, Murphy and Murray dealt with such topics as the Eucharist and Christ's love and compassion, the Eucharist and liberation, and the Eucharist and Resurrection and hope respectively.

In conjunction with each of the weekend lectures a follow-up session was arranged on the following Thursday night in the school hall. This was organised and presided over by Sister Theophane of Rockford Manor. The priest who lectured on the previous weekend attended and there was an opportunity for an informal exchange on matters arising from his address or anything relevant to the Eucharist and the Mass.

The numbers who heard the lectures on the Eucharist on the various weekends ranged from three-and-a-half to four thousand. Reaction was generally very favourable. The various lectures presented a good measure of variety of style and content and this, it seems, helped to retain the attention on the congregation. Any criticism there was was directed at Professor Marsh's contribution. There were complaints that it was too academic, too abstract and too far advanced. However, quite a number of people considered it to be by far the best of the lectures. The follow-up sessions in the school hall were less successful. The average attendance was 31. This, despite the fact of the parish having hundreds of generous and committed persons:

75 Eucharistic ministers,
20 readers,
a 25-strong choir,
a Carmelite group,
a branch of the Legion of Mary,
a prayer group,
a Vincent de Paul Conference,
Boy scouts,
Majorettes, etc.

Moreover, in the parish newsletter and from the pulpit, parishioners were urged to attend these sessions if at all possible. The attendance was disappointing in the light of the excellent manner in which sessions were conducted by Sister Theophane. A further feature was the fact that no-one under the age of 50 attended, reflecting a reluctance on the part of persons under that age to devote weekday evenings to such matters.

The attempt to implement the Eucharist Renewal programme highlighted a number of truisms:

(1) How essential it is to utilise to the full the presence, attention and goodwill of the Sunday Mass congregations to
deepen the knowledge of the Faith of the parishioners;

(2) How difficult it is to persuade parishioners, apart from a
relative few, to attend discussions, talks, lectures on religious
topics;

(3) That it would be well nigh impossible to organise and sustain religion classes for a substantial number of children of
practically any parish, apart from the Catholic primary and
secondary schools;

(4) That the access we now enjoy to the schools is vitally
important and should be used to the full.

On this last point there has been considerable discussion in recent years. It is felt by some people that the catechesis in the
schools is not achieving satisfactory results. Few of its products
seem to be able to articulate the fundamentals of their faith.
Protagonists of the present programmes argue that they succeed
in conveying a proper attitude to the Faith. While such an attitude is important, the capacity to express one's faith is at least
equally important.

The challenge to improve the standard of catechetical in-
struction is formidable. It is a task for the specialists but not only
for them. Perhaps the best persons to be entrusted with overall
responsibility for this would be a representative committee of
the country's diocesan examiners. In the meantime a number of
initiatives could be taken:

(1) Those of us who are chaplains to schools during the
course of our regular visits to classes should use the entire
class period teaching. Subjects that could and should be
taught at all levels are: the Mass, the Sacraments, the
Commandments, the Our Father and Hail Mary and, above
all, the importance of Sunday Mass and prayer;

(2) Diocesan examiners should examine;

(3) There should be an immediate, in-depth appraisal of the content of the catechetical courses now in use;

(4) There ought to be greater awareness and appreciation by those engaged in pastoral work of the difficulties facing those involved in developing a catechesis which will be effective in the ethos obtaining today.

Link Up, July 1990

Index of Persons

à Kempis, Thomas (author) 12
Adenauer, Konrad (chancellor) 135
Ahern, Rev Professor John (later bishop) 28
Aherne, Rev Patrick (later parish priest, Knocknagoshel) 31
Aiken, James (entertainments promoter) 30
Alexander VI (pope) 123
Alston CC, Fr James (later parish priest, Swords) 129
Anderdon SJ, Fr William 153
Andrews TD, David (later foreign minister) 119
    Eamonn (broadcaster, later head of RTE) 133
    TD, Niall 119
Archdeacon CC, Fr John 162-3, 167
Aristotle (philosopher) 16
Ayer, A. J. (logical positivist) 16

Baker CC, Fr John (later parish priest, Dolphin's Barn) 41-2
Ball, Francis Elrington (historian) 159-60
Banks, James (pianist) 95
Barbarolli, Sir John 29
Barrett, Thomas (sacristan) 92-3
Barry, Kevin (IRA) 106
Barry PP, Very Rev Thomas 106-7, 109, 112-13, 123
Bassett SJ, Fr Bernard 154
Bates, Peter (St Vincent de Paul conference) 109
Bergin CC, Fr Denis (later parish priest, Blackrock) 126-7
Betham, Sir William 165
Birch, Rev Professor Peter (later bishop) 26
Black, Rev Desmond (rector) 130
Blaney TD, Neil 119
Bodkin, Mrs Thomas P. (wife of director, National Gallery of Ireland) 111
Booker, Harry (IRFU) 131
    Mrs Rhona (wife of Harry) 131
Boski, Jan (stock exchange trader) 173
Bossuet, Bishop Jacques Benigne 26
Brady, Peter (drummer) 95
Breen CC, Fr Liam (later parish priest, Arklow) 40-1
Britain, Matthew (Bray Emmets GFC) 47
Broderick, Mrs Elizabeth (grandmother of J. Anthony Gaughan) 10
    Kathleen (later Mrs Anthony Gaughan) 9
Brodrick SJ, Fr James 154
Brooks, Sister Vincent (Daughters of Charity) 83-4

Forde, Sheila (school principal, later Mrs Green) 108
Freud, Sigmund (psychologist) 16
Fullenbach, Fr John (theologian) 178
Fuller, Hubert (youth leader) 187

Gallagher, Fr Colm CC (later parish priest, Arklow) 69
        Vincent (architect) 69
Gallen, Rev Professor Edward (vice-president, Holy Cross College,
        Clonliffe) 17
Garry, Thomas (school principal) 164
Gaughan, Anthony (army officer, civil servant) 9
        Michael (hunger-striker) 121
Gibbon, Edward (historian) 177
Gilmore, Thomas (teacher) 92
Greehy, Fr John J. (later Mgr and president, Clonliffe College) 45
Greene, Fr Stephen CC (later Mgr and head of National Marriage
        Appeals Tribunal) 50, 53-5
Gregan, Francis (co-founder, Monkstown Credit Union) 111
Gregory VII (pope) 25
Greiswood, Frederick (broadcaster) 178
Griffith PP, Very Rev Andrew 111
Guinness, Mrs Peggy (wife of Ralph) 121-3
        Ralph (prop., 'Punch Bowl') 121

Hamell, Rev Professor Patrick Joseph (later Mgr and parish priest, Birr) 24
Hannafin, Mrs Mona (promoter of devotion to Padre Pio) 85
Hanney, Michael (fireman) 120
        Mrs Rita (wife of Michael) 120
Harold, Mrs Kathleen (sister of Mrs Peggy Guinness) 122-3
Harty, Rev Professor Michael (later bishop) 28
Hayes, Fr Frederick CC (later parish priest, Bluebell) 41
Heath MP, Edward (prime minister) 135
Heenan, Fr John Carmel (Catholic Missionary Soc., later cardinal) 154
Hegarty, Fr Edward CC 114
        Fr Rex CC 106, 108, 112-15, 123
Henry IV (German emperor) 25
Henry PP, Very Rev George 60-6, 68, 138
Herrema, Tiede (businessman) 120
Higgins, John (prop., Rockford Manor) 165
Hipwell, Canon Trevor (rector) 131
Hislop OP, Fr Ian 154
Hogan, Fr Joseph (later parish priest, Castledermot) 45
Hooke PP, Very Rev Frederick 86-7
Hooper, Dr Barry (GP) 104
Hopkins, Hilary (St Vincent de Paul Society) 119
Horgan TD, John 136-7
        Mgr John D. (professor) 16, 71, 76

Howell SJ, Fr Clifford 38
Howett CC, Fr Desmond 60
Hume, Cardinal Basil 178
Hume Dudgeon, Lt Col 165
Hungerford Pollen, John (architect) 143
Hurley, Mgr Charles 65-6
    Fr Timothy CC (later parish priest, Kilquade) 162-3, 165-7
Hurwitz, Cecil (author and peace campaigner) 174-5
Hyland, Mark (Dún Laoghaire Corporation) 118
Hynes, Desmond (prop., 'O'Donoghues', Merrion Row) 119

John Paul II (pope) 152, 179
Johnson OSB, Fr Dominic 133-5
Johnston CC, Fr Cecil (later parish priest, Cabra West) 51-3, 56
    Mrs Rita (Fr Johnston's housekeeper) 51
Jonah (prophet) 25
Jones CSsR, Rev Professor Frederick 188
Judas Iscariot 95
Jung, Carl Gustav (psychologist) 16

Kane PP, Very Rev Walter 64-5
Kavanagh, Fr James (later bishop) 40
    Very Rev John PP 69
Kavanagh CC, Fr John ('Flash') 53
Keane, Ronan (judge) 15
Keating, Mary (lecturer) 173-4
Kelly CC, Fr Brian (later parish priest, Howth) 47
    Brother James (Irish Christian Brothers) 129
    Canon John (president, Holy Cross College, Clonliffe) 11, 17, 132
    Fr Thomas SM 75
Kemmis, Captain William (landlord) 70
Kennelly, Michael (scoutmaster) 10
Kenyon PP, Very Rev John 161
Kickham, Charles J. (author) 161
Kilcullen, Justin (Trocáire) 130
    Mrs Maura (Mt Merrion) 130
Killanin, Lord 155
Kirley, Joseph (photographer) 97
Kisner ASC, Sister Madeleine 156-7
Kissane, Mgr Edward J. (president, Maynooth College) 29
    Seán (army officer) 10
Knox, Mgr Ronald 154

Lacordaire OP, Fr Jean Baptiste Henri 184
Lane CC, Fr Dermot (later parish priest, Balally, and president Mater Dei Institute of Education) 127
Lawless CC, Fr Bennie (later parish priest, Aughrim Street) 154, 156
Leahy, Rev Professor Michael Joseph (later parish priest) 24-5